Fromm, Erich, 1 00

BF85   Greatness and
F753   limitations of
        Freud's thought

DATE		
FEB 21 '83	NOV 1 6 2000	
MAY 6 '93	APR 0 1 2002	
AUG 2 5 1989	MAY 2 1 2002	
JAN 8 0 1990		
FEB 1 9		
JAN 1 3		
APR 1 3 '92		
DEC 1 4 1998		
MAR 0 3 1999		

APR 1 5 2003

GREATNESS AND LIMITATIONS OF FREUD'S THOUGHT

Also By Erich Fromm:

Marx's Concept of Man
Man for Himself
Psychoanalysis and Religion
The Forgotten Language
The Sane Society
The Art of Loving
Sigmund Freud's Mission
Escape from Freedom
The Dogma of Christ and Other Essays on Religion,
    Psychology and Culture
You Shall Be as Gods: A Radical Interpretation of
    the Old Testament and Its Traditions
The Revolution of Hope
Beyond the Chains of Illusion
The Heart of Man
The Anatomy of Human Destructiveness
To Have or to Be?
The Crisis of Psychoanalysis
May Man Prevail?
Social Character in a Mexican Village
Zen Buddhism and Psychoanalysis

Harper & Row, Publishers

New York

Cambridge
Hagerstown
Philadelphia
San Francisco

1817

London
Mexico City
São Paulo
Sydney

GREATNESS AND LIMITATIONS OF FREUD'S THOUGHT

Erich Fromm

This work was first published in Germany under the title
Sigmund Freuds Psychoanalyse—Grösse und Grenzen in 1979 by
Deutsche Verlags-Anstalt.

GREATNESS AND LIMITATIONS OF FREUD'S THOUGHT. Copyright
© 1980 by The Estate of Erich Fromm. All rights reserved.
Printed in the United States of America. No part of this book
may be used or reproduced in any manner whatsoever without written permission except in the case of brief quotations
embodied in critical articles and reviews. For information
address Harper & Row, Publishers, Inc., 10 East 53rd Street,
New York, N.Y. 10022. Published simultaneously in Canada
by Fitzhenry & Whiteside Limited, Toronto.

FIRST EDITION

Designer: Gloria Adelson

Library of Congress Cataloging in Publication Data

Fromm, Erich, 1900–
   Greatness and limitations of Freud's thought.
   Bibliography: p.
   Includes index.
   1. Freud, Sigmund, 1856–1939. 2. Psychoanalysis.
I. Title.
BF173.F85F753   150.19'52   79–2730
ISBN 0–06–011389–8

80 81 82 83 84 10 9 8 7 6 5 4 3 2 1

Contents

Contents

Preface

In order to appreciate fully the extraordinary significance of
Freud's psychoanalytic discoveries, one must start out with understanding the principle on which they are based, and one cannot express this principle more adequately than through the
sentence of the Gospels "And the truth shall make you free"
(John 8:32). Indeed, the idea that the truth saves and heals is an
old insight which the great Masters of Living have proclaimed—
nobody perhaps with such radicalism and clarity as the Buddha,
yet it is a thought common to Judaism and Christianity, to Socra-
tes, Spinoza, Hegel and Marx.

For Buddhist thought, illusion (ignorance) is, together with
hate and greed, one of the evils of which man must rid himself
if he does not want to remain in a state of craving which necessarily causes suffering. Buddhism does not combat joy or even pleasure in the world, provided it is not the result of craving and
greed. The greedy man cannot be a free man and cannot be a
happy man. He is a slave of things which rule him. The process

of waking up from illusions is the condition of freedom and of liberation from suffering which greed necessarily produces. Disillusion *(Ent-täuschung)* is a condition for leading a life which comes closest to the full development of man, or in Spinoza's words, to the model of human nature. Less central and radical, because tainted with the idea of a God-idol, is the concept of truth, and the need for disillusionment in the Christian and Jewish traditions. But when these religions compromised with power, they could not help betraying truth. In the revolutionary sects, truth could have a prominent place again because their whole thrust was that of uncovering the contradiction between Christian thought and Christian practice.

Spinoza's teachings in many ways resemble those of the Buddha. The human being who is carried away by irrational drives ("passive affects") is necessarily one who has inadequate ideas about himself and the world—that is to say, one who lives with illusions. Those who are guided by reason are the ones who have ceased to be seduced by their senses and follow the two "active affects," reason and courage. Marx is in the tradition of those for whom truth is the condition for salvation. His whole work was not primarily that of showing a picture of how the good society would look, but was a relentless critique of illusions which prevent man from building the good society. As Marx put it, one must destroy illusions in order to change circumstances which require illusions.

Freud could have formulated the same sentence as a fitting motto for a therapy based on psychoanalytic theory. He enlarged the concept of truth tremendously. For him truth referred not only to what one believes or one thinks consciously, but also to what one represses because one does not wish to think it.

The greatness of Freud's discovery consists in the fact that he conceived a method of arriving at the truth beyond that which an individual believes to be the truth, and he could do that due to having discovered the effects of repression, and correspondingly, rationalizations. He demonstrated empirically that the way to cure lies in insight into one's own mental structure and thereby in "de-repression." This application of the principle that truth liberates and cures is perhaps the greatest achievement of Freud, even though his application of this principle underwent many distortions and often produced new illusions.

In this book I want to present the most important discoveries of Freud, in detailed form. At the same time I shall try to show where and in what way bourgeois thought, so characteristic of Freud, narrowed down and sometimes even obscured his discoveries. Since my critique of Freud has its own continuity, I cannot avoid referring back to earlier statements I have made on the subject.

ERICH FROMM

1. The Limitations of Scientific Knowledge

The attempt to understand Freud's theoretical system, or that of any creative systematic thinker, cannot be successful unless we recognize that, and why, every system as it is developed and presented by its author is *necessarily* erroneous. That is so not because of the lack of ingenuity, creativeness or self-criticism on the part of the author, but because of a fundamental and unavoidable contradiction: on the one hand the author has something new to say, something that has not been thought or said before. But in speaking of "newness" one places it only into a descriptive category which does not do justice to what is essential in the creative thought. The creative thought is always a *critical* thought because it does away with certain illusion and gets closer to the awareness of reality. It enlarges the realm of man's awareness and strengthens the power of his reason. The critical and hence creative thought always has a liberating function by its negation of illusory thought.

On the other hand the thinker has to *express* his new thought in the spirit of his time. Different societies have different kinds of "common sense," different categories of thinking, different systems of logic; every society has its own "social filter" through which only certain ideas and concepts and experiences can pass; those that need not necessarily remain unconscious can become conscious when by fundamental changes in the social structure the "social filter" changes accordingly. Thoughts that cannot pass through the social filter of a certain society at a certain time are "unthinkable," and of course also "unspeakable." For the average person the thought patterns of his society appear to be simply logical. The thought patterns of fundamentally different societies are looked upon each by the other as illogical or plainly nonsensical. But not only "logic" is determined by the "social filter," and in the last analysis by the practice of life of any given society, but also certain thought contents. Take for instance the conventional notion that exploitation among human beings is a "normal," natural and unavoidable phenomenon. For a member of the Neolithic society in which each man and woman lived from his or her work, individually or in groups, such a proposition would have been unthinkable. Considering their whole social organization, exploitation of human beings by others would have been a "crazy" idea, because there was not yet a surplus to make it sensible to employ others. (If one person had forced another to work for him it would not have meant that the amount of goods would have increased, only that the "employer" would have been forced to idleness and boredom.) Another example: the many societies that knew no private property in the modern sense but only "functional property," like a tool, which "belonged" to a single person inasmuch as he used it but was readily shared with others when needed.

What is unthinkable is also unspeakable and the language has no word for it. Many languages do not have a word for *to have* but must express the concept of possession in other words, for instance by the construction *it is to me*, which expresses the concept of functional but not of private property ("private" in the sense of the Latin *privare*, to deprive—that is to say, property the use of which everybody else is deprived of except the owner). Many languages started out without a word for *to have* but in their development and, one may assume, with the emergence of private property, they acquired a word for it (see Benveniste, 1966). Another example: in the tenth or eleventh century in Europe the concept of the world without reference to God was unthinkable and hence a word like *atheism* could not exist. Language itself is influenced by the social repression of certain experiences which do not fit into the structure of a given society; languages differ inasmuch as different experiences are repressed, and hence inexpressible.*

It follows that the creative thinker must think in the terms of the logic, the thought patterns, the expressible concepts of his culture. That means he has not yet the proper words to express the creative, the new, the liberating idea. He is forced to solve an insoluble problem: to express the new thought in concepts and words that do not yet exist in his language. (They may very well exist at a later time when his creative thoughts have been generally accepted.) The consequence is that the new thought as he formulated it is a blend of what is truly new and the conventional thought which it transcends. The thinker, however, is not conscious of this contradiction. The conventional thoughts of his culture are unquestionably true for him and hence he himself is little aware of the difference between what is creative in his thought and what is purely conventional. Only in the historical process, when social changes are reflected in the changes of thought patterns, does it become evident what in the thought of

*I leave aside here quite a different problem, that of the possibility of expressing subtle and complex feeling experiences through language, which can be attempted only in poetry.

a creative thinker was truly new and to what extent his system is only a reflection of conventional thinking. It is up to his followers living in a different frame of ideas to interpret the "master" by distinguishing his "original" thoughts from his conventional thoughts, and by analyzing the contradictions between the new and the old, rather than by trying to harmonize the immanent contradictions of his system by all kinds of subterfuge.

The process of revision of an author, which distinguishes the essential and new from the contingent, time-conditioned elements, is in itself also the product of a certain historical period that influences the interpretation. In this creative interpretation, again creative and valid elements are mixed with time-bound and accidental ones. The revision is not simply true as the original was not simply false. Some elements of the revision remain true, namely where it liberates the theory from the shackles of a previous conventional thinking. In the process of the critical elimination of previous theories we find an approximation to truth but we do not find the truth, and we cannot find the truth as long as social contradictions and force require ideological falsification, as long as man's reason is damaged by irrational passions which have their root in the disharmony and irrationality of social life. Only in a society in which there is no exploitation, hence which does not need irrational assumptions in order to cover up or justify exploitation, in a society in which the basic contradictions have been solved and in which social reality can be recognized without distortion, can man make full use of his reason, and at that point he can recognize reality in an undistorted form—that is to say, the truth. To put it differently, the truth is historically conditioned: it is dependent on the degree of rationality and the absence of contradictions within the society.

Man can grasp truth only when he can regulate his social life in a human, dignified and rational way, without fear and hence without greed. To use a politico-religious expression, only in the Messianic Time can the truth be recognized insofar as it is recognizable.

THE ROOTS OF FREUD'S ERRORS

Applying this principle to Freud's thinking means that to understand Freud one must try to recognize which of his findings were truly new and creative, to what extent he had to express them in a distorted way and how by liberating his ideas from these shackles his discoveries become all the more fruitful.

Referring to what has been said in general about Freud's thought, the question arises, What was truly unthinkable to Freud and hence a "roadblock" beyond which he could not go?

If we try to answer the question What was really unthinkable for Freud? I can see only two complexes:

1. The theory of bourgeois materialism, especially as it was developed in Germany by men like Vogt, Moleschott and Büchner. In *Kraft und Stoff (Force and Matter)* (1855) Büchner claimed to have discovered that there is no force without matter and no matter without force; this dogma was widely accepted in Freud's time. The dogma of bourgeois materialism expressed by Freud was that of his teachers, especially his most important teacher, von Brücke. Freud remained strongly under the influence of the thinking of von Brücke and of bourgeois materialism in general, and under this influence he could not conceive that there could be strong psychical powers whose specific physiological roots could not be demonstrated.

Freud's real aim was to understand human passions; previously the philosophers, playwrights and novelists—not the psychologists or neurologists—were concerned with the passions.

How did Freud solve the problem? At a time when relatively little was known about hormonal influences on the psyche there was indeed one phenomenon in which the connection of the physiological and the psychical was well known: sexuality. If one considered sexuality as the root of all drives, then the theoretical demand was satisfied, the physiological roots of psychic forces were discovered. It was Jung who later cut loose from this connection, and in this respect made, as I see it, a truly valuable addition to Freud's thought.

2. The second complex of unthinkable thoughts had to do with Freud's bourgeois and authoritarian-patriarchal attitude. A society in which women were truly equal to men, in which men did not rule because of their alleged physiological and psychical superiority, was simply unthinkable for Freud. When John Stuart Mill, whom Freud admired a great deal, expressed his ideas concerning the equality of women, Freud wrote in a letter, "On this point Mill is simply crazy." The word *crazy* is typical for defining that which is unthinkable. Most people call certain ideas "crazy" because "sane" is only that which is within the frame of reference of conventional thought. That which transcends it is crazy in the view of the average person. (This, however, is different when the author, or artist, becomes successful. Does not success certify sanity?) That the equality of women was unthinkable to Freud led him to his psychology of women. I believe that his concept that half of mankind is biologically, anatomically and psychically inferior to the other half is the only idea in his thinking which seems to be without the slightest redeeming feature, except as a portrayal of a male-chauvinistic attitude.

But the bourgeois character of Freud's thought is by no means only to be found in this extreme form of patriarchalism. Indeed there are few thinkers who are "radical" in the sense of transcending the thinking of their class. Freud was not one of them. The class background and his manner of thinking show in virtually all his theoretical statements. Since he was not a radical thinker, how could it be otherwise? Indeed there would be nothing to complain about, were it not for the fact that his orthodox (and unorthodox) followers were encouraged in their uncritical attitude toward society. This attitude of Freud's also explains why his creation, which was a critical theory, namely the critique of human consciousness, hardly brought forward any more than a handful of radical political thinkers.

It would be necessary to write a whole book if one wanted to analyze Freud's most important concepts and theories from the standpoint of their class origin.* It certainly cannot be done within the framework of this book. However, here are three examples.

1. Freud's therapeutic aim was control of instinctual drives through the strengthening of the ego; they have to be subdued by ego and superego. In the latter respect Freud is close to medieval theological thought, although with the important difference that in his system there is no place for grace or for motherly love, beyond that of feeding the child. The key word is *control.*

The psychological concept corresponds to the social reality. Just as socially the majority is controlled by a ruling minority, the psyche is supposed to be controlled by the authority of the ego and superego. The danger of the breakthrough of the unconscious carries with it the danger of a social revolution. Repression is a repressive authoritarian method of protecting the inner and outer status quo. It is by no means the only way to cope with problems of social change. But the threat of force in keeping down what is "dangerous" is only necessary in an authoritarian system where the preservation of the status quo is the supreme goal. Other models of individual and social structures can be experimented with. In the last analysis the question is How much renunciation of happiness does the ruling minority in a society need to impose on the majority? The answer lies in the development of productive forces in the society, and hence in the degree to which the individual is necessarily frustrated. The whole scheme "superego, ego, id" is a hierarchical structure, which excludes the possibility that the association of free, i.e., nonexploited, human beings can live harmoniously and without the necessity of controlling sinister forces.

2. It goes without saying that Freud's grotesque picture of

*Of course not all class elements in Freud's thinking are necessarily exclusively of "bourgeois" origin. Some are common to all patriarchal societies centered on private property.

women (cf. lecture 33 in Freud, 1933a) as essentially narcissistic, unable to love and sexually cool is male propaganda. The middle-class woman was as a rule sexually cold. The proprietary character of bourgeois marriage conditioned them to be cold. Since they were property, they were expected to be "inanimate" in marriage. Only women of the upper class and courtesans were permitted to be active sexual subjects (or at least to fake it). No wonder that men experienced lust in the process of conquest; the overevaluation of the "sexual object" which according to Freud existed only in men (another lack in women!) was, as far as I can see, essentially the pleasure in the chase and the eventual conquest. Once the conquest was assured by the first intercourse, the woman was relegated to the task of producing children and to being an efficient housekeeper; she had changed from an object of chase to a no-person.* If Freud had had many female patients from the highest classes of French and English aristocracy, his rigid picture of the cold woman might have changed.

3. Perhaps the most important example of the bourgeois qualities of Freud's seemingly universal concepts is that of love. Indeed, Freud speaks of love, more than his orthodox followers are accustomed to do. But what does he mean by love?

It is most important to note that Freud and his disciples usually speak of "object love" (in contrast to "narcissistic love") and of a "love-object" (meaning the person one loves). Is there really such a thing as a "love-object"? Does not the loved person cease to be an object, i.e., something outside and opposed to me (same root as in *to object*)? Is not love precisely the inner activity which unites two people so that they cease to be objects (i.e., possessions for each other)? To speak of love-objects is to speak of having, with exclusion of any form of being (see Fromm, 1976a); it is not different from a merchant speaking of capital investment.

---

*All this is clearly demonstrated in Freud's own marriage: excited, romantic love letters, largely the narcissistic image of the great lover so typical of nineteenth-century love letters, until the marriage; afterward a marked lack of interest in her erotically, intellectually and affectively.

In the latter case capital is invested, in the former, libido. It is only logical that frequently in psychoanalytic literature one speaks of love as libidinous "investment" in an object. It takes the banality of a business culture to reduce the love of God, of men and women, of mankind to an investment; or the enthusiasm of a Rumi, Eckhart, Shakespeare, Schweitzer to show the smallness of the imagination of people whose class considers investment and profit to be the very meaning of life.

From his theoretic premises Freud is forced to speak of love-"objects," since "libido remains libido whether it is directed to objects or to one's own ego" (Freud, 1916–17, p. 420). Love is sexual energy attached to an object; it is nothing but a physiologically rooted instinct directed toward an object. It is a waste product, as it were, of the biological necessity for the survival of the race. "Love," in men, is mostly of the "attachment" type, i.e., attachment to the persons who have become precious through satisfying other vital needs (eating and drinking). That is, adult love is not different from that of the child; they both love those who feed them. This is undoubtedly true for many; this love is a kind of affectionate gratitude for being fed. Very well, but to say that is the essence of love is painfully banal. (Women, as he says in Freud, 1933a, p. 132f., cannot arrive at this high achievement because they love "narcissistically," they love themselves in the other.)

Freud postulates: "Loving in itself, insofar as it is longing and deprivation, lowers self-regard, whereas being loved, having one's love returned and *possessing the loved object* raises it once more" (Freud, 1914c, p. 99, italics added). This statement is a key to the understanding of Freud's concept of love. Loving, implying longing and deprivation, lowers one's self-regard. To those who proclaimed the exaltation and strength which loving gives to the lover, Freud said: All of you are wrong! *Loving* makes you weak; what makes you happy is *being loved.* And what is being loved? *Possessing* the loved object! This is a classic definition of bourgeois love: owning and controlling makes for happiness, be it material property or be it a woman who, being owned, owes the owner love. Love begins as a result of the child being fed by mother. It ends in the male's owning the female who still has to feed him with affection, sexual pleasure and food. Here we find perhaps the key to the concept of the Oedipus complex. By setting up the straw man of incest Freud hides what he considers to be the essence of the male's love: the eternal attachment to a mother who feeds and at the same time is controlled by the male. Indeed what Freud says between the lines is probably fitting for patriarchal societies: the male remains a dependent creature but denies this by boasting of his strength and proving it through making the female his property.

To sum up: the main factors in the patriarchal male's attitude are dependence on the female and its denial by controlling her. Freud, as so often, has transformed a specific phenomenon, that of patriarchal male love, into a universal human one.

THE PROBLEM OF SCIENTIFIC "TRUTH"

It has become fashionable today to say, and practitioners of various branches of academic psychology are particularly prone to make this point, that Freud's theory is "unscientific." This statement of course depends entirely on what one calls the scientific method. Many psychologists and sociologists have a rather naïve concept of the scientific method. Briefly speaking, it consists in the expectation that first one gathers facts, one puts these facts through modes of quantitative measurements—computers have made that extremely easy—and then one expects that as a result of these efforts one will arrive at a theory or at least a hypothesis. The further assumption then is that, as in an experiment in the natural sciences, the truth of the theory depends on the possibility of the experiment being repeated by others, always with the same results. Problems which do not lend themselves to this kind of quantification and statistical approach are supposed to be of a nonscientific character and hence outside the field of scientific psychology. In this scheme, one or two or three instances which permit the observer to arrive at certain definitive conclusions are declared to be more or less worthless if a considerable number of instances cannot be produced which fit a statistical procedure. Essential to this concept of the scientific method is the tacit assumption that the facts themselves produce the theory if only the proper method is employed and that the role of creative thinking by the observer is very small. What is required from him is the capacity to arrange a seemingly satisfactory experiment without starting with a theory of his own which he may prove or disprove in the course of the experiment. This concept of science as a simple sequence of selected facts, experiment and certainty of the result is dated, and it is significant that the real scientists today, such as physicists, biologists, chemists, astronomers, have long given up this kind of primitive concept of the scientific method.

What distinguishes the creative from the pseudo-scientists today is the belief in the potency of reason, the belief that human reason and human imagination can penetrate the deceptive surface of the phenomena and arrive at hypotheses that deal with the underlying forces rather than the surface. It is essential that the last thing they expect is certainty. They know that every hypothesis will be replaced by another one which does not necessarily negate the first but modifies and enlarges it.

The scientist can stand this uncertainty precisely because of his faith in human reason. What matters to him is not to arrive at a conclusion but to reduce the degree of illusion, to penetrate deeper to the roots. The scientist is not even afraid of being wrong; he knows that the history of science is a history of erroneous but productive, pregnant statements from which new insights are born that overcome the relative wrongness of the older statement and lead to new insights. If scientists were obsessed by the wish not to be wrong, they would never have arrived at insights which are relatively right. Of course if the social scientist has only trivial questions and does not turn his attention to fundamental problems, his "scientific method" achieves results sufficient for the endless papers which he needs to write in order to promote his academic career.

This has by no means always been the method of social scientists. One need only think of men like Marx, Durkheim, Mayo, Max and Alfred Weber, Tönnies. They addressed themselves to the most fundamental problems and their answers were not based on the naïve and positivistic method of relying on statistical results as theory-creating. For them the power of reason and the belief in this power was just as strong and significant as it was in the most outstanding natural scientists. But in social sciences things have changed. With the increasing power of big industry, many social scientists submit and deal mainly with problems that can be solved without disturbing the system.

What is the procedure today which constitutes the scientific method both in the natural sciences and in legitimate social science?

1. The scientist does not start out from nothing, rather his thinking is determined by his previous knowledge and by the challenge of unexplored areas.

2. Most minute and detailed exploration of phenomena is the condition of optimal objectivity. It is characteristic of the scientist that he has the greatest respect for the observable phenomena; many great discoveries have been made because a scientist paid attention to a small event which was seen but ignored by everybody else.

3. On the basis of the known theories and the optimum of detailed knowledge, he formulates a hypothesis. The function of a hypothesis should be to bring some order to the observed phenomena and to arrange them tentatively in such a way that they seem to make some sense. It is also essential that the researcher is capable at every moment of observing new data which may contradict his hypothesis and lead to its revision and so *ad infinitum.*

4. This scientific method requires of course that the scientist

is at least relatively free from wishful and narcissistic thinking; that is to say, that he can observe the facts objectively without distorting them or giving them inadequate weight because he is so eager to prove that his hypothesis is right. The combination of wide-ranging imagination and objectivity is seldom reached and this is probably the reason why great scientists, who would have to fulfill both conditions, are rare. High intelligence is necessary but is not by itself sufficient for becoming a creative scientist. In fact a condition of complete objectivity can hardly ever be fully achieved. In the first place the scientist, as we have discussed, always is influenced by the common sense of his time, and furthermore only extraordinary persons of great gift are immune from narcissism. Yet altogether the discipline of scientific thinking has produced a degree of objectivity and what one might call scientific conscience that is hardly matched in other areas of cultural life. Indeed the fact that the great scientists more than anybody else have seen the dangers threatening mankind today and warned of them is the expression of their capacity to be objective and unswayed by the clamor of misguided public opinion.

These principles of the scientific method—objectivity, observation, hypothesis formation and revision by further study of facts, while valid for all scientific endeavor, cannot be applied in the same way to all objects of scientific thought. While I am not competent to speak about physics there is undoubtedly a marked difference between the observation of a person as a whole and alive and the observation of certain aspects (of a personality) that one has separated from the total personality and studies without reference to this whole. This cannot be done in any system without distorting those isolated aspects which one tries to study, because they are in constant interaction with every other part of the system and cannot be understood outside of the whole. If one tries to study one aspect of a personality apart from the whole, one has to dissect the person—that is to say, destroy his wholeness. Then one can examine this or that isolated aspect but all the results one arrives at are necessarily false because they are gained from dead material, the dissected man.

The living person can be understood only as a whole and in his aliveness, in the constant process of change. Since every individual is different from any other, even the possibility of generalizations and the formulation of laws is limited, though the scientific observer will always try to find some general principles and laws in the manifoldness of individuals.

There is another difficulty in the scientific approach to the understanding of man. The data which we obtain from a person are unlike the data we obtain in other scientific endeavors. One has to understand man in his full subjectivity to understand him at all. A word is not "a" word because a word is that which it means to a certain person who uses it. The dictionary meaning of the word is only an abstraction compared to the real meaning which a word has for the person who pronounces it. That of course is irrelevant for words for physical objects, although not entirely, but it is relevant for words referring to emotional or intellectual experiences. A love letter from the beginning of the century sounds to us sentimental, contrived and kind of silly. A love letter from our time which wanted to convey the same sentiments would have appeared to people living fifty years ago as cold and feelingless. The words *love, faith, courage, hate* have an entirely subjective meaning for every individual and it is no exaggeration to say that it is never the same meaning for two people because there are no two people who are identical. It may not have even the same meaning for one person that it had ten years earlier because of the changes that he or she has undergone. The same holds true of course for dreams. Two dreams which are identical in their content may still have two very different meanings for two different dreamers.

One of the important points in Freud's scientific approach was precisely his knowledge of the subjectivity of human utterances. On this knowledge he based his attempt not to take a word a person uttered for granted, but to raise the question of what this particular word at this particular moment in this particular context meant for this particular person. This subjectivity in fact enhances the objectivity of Freud's method considerably. Any psychologist who is naïve enough to think "a word is a word is a word" will communicate with another person only on a highly abstract and fictitious level. A word is a sign for a unique experience.

Freud's Scientific Method

If we understand by the scientific method a method based on the belief in the potency of reason optimally free from subjective prejudices, detailed observation of facts, formation of hypotheses, revision of the hypotheses by the discovery of new facts, et cetera, we can see that Freud certainly was a scientist. He adapted his scientific method to the necessity of studying the irrational rather than only what can be studied with a positivistic concept of science, as most social scientists do. Another important aspect of Freud's thinking is that he saw his object in terms of a system or structure and that he offered one of the earliest examples of System Theory. In his view no single element in a personality can be understood without understanding the whole, and no single element can be changed without changes occurring, even to a minute degree, in other elements of the system. Unlike the viewpoint of a positivistic dissecting kind of psychology, and very much like that of older psychological systems, as for instance those of Spinoza, Freud's considered the individual as a whole and as more than a summation of parts.

So far we have talked about the scientific method and its positive meaning. But in merely describing the scientific method of a thinker one does not necessarily mean that he was correct in his results. Indeed, the history of scientific thought is a history of pregnant errors.

Here is just one example of Freud's scientific approach, his report on the case of Dora. Freud treated this patient for hysteria and after three months the analysis came to an end. Without going into the details of Freud's presentation I want to show his objective attitude by quoting from the case history. The patient opened the third session with these words:

> "Do you know that I am here for the last time today?"—"How can I know, as you have said nothing to me about it?"—"Yes, I made up my mind to put up with it till the New Year. (It was December 31st.) But I shall wait no longer than that to be cured."—"You know that you are free to stop the treatment at any time. But for today we will go on with our work. When did you come to this decision?"—"A fortnight ago, I think."—"That sounds just like a maidservant or a governess—a fortnight's warning."—"There was a governess who gave warning with the K.'s, when I was on my visit to them that time at L——, by the lake."—"Really? You have never told me about her. Tell me" (Freud, 1905e, p. 105).

Freud then spent the rest of the session analyzing what this acting out of the role of a maidservant really meant. It does not matter here to what conclusions Freud came; what matters is the purity of his scientific approach. He does not get angry, he does not ask the patient to reconsider, does not encourage her by saying that if she stays working with him she will improve; he only states that since she is with him, even though it is one of the last sessions, they may as well use the time to understand what her decision means.

But with all admiration for Freud's faith in reason, and in the scientific method, it cannot be denied that Freud often gives us the picture of an obsessive rationalist who constructs theories on the basis of practically nothing, and does violence to reason. He often made constructions using scraps of evidence that led to conclusions which were nothing short of absurd. I refer to Freud's case history from *The History of an Infantile Neurosis.* * As

---

*(Freud, 1918b. Freud finished the case history in November 1914, but held back its publication for four years.) The case is popularly known as the Report on the Wolf Man. (See also the most interesting compilation edited by Muriel Gardiner, *The Wolf-Man by the Wolf-Man,* in which she includes an autobiography of the Wolf Man, Freud's case history and a supplement by Ruth Mack Brunswick.)

Freud himself remarks, when he wrote the report he was still freshly under the impression of what he called "twisted reinter-pretation" of psychoanalysis by C. G. Jung and Alfred Adler. In order to explain what I mean in referring to Freud's obsessional thinking, I must go into this report at some length.

What are the essential facts and problems in this case?

In 1910 an extremely wealthy young Russian came to Freud for help. The treatment lasted until July 1914 when Freud regarded the case as completed and wrote the history. Freud reports that the patient "had lived an approximately normal life during the ten years of his boyhood that preceded the date of his illness, and got through his studies at his secondary school without much trouble. But his earlier years were dominated by a severe neurotic disturbance which began immediately before his fourth birthday as an anxiety-hysteria (in the shape of an animal phobia) then changed into an obsessional neurosis with a religious content, and lasted with its offshoots as far as into his tenth year" (Freud, 1918b, pp. 8–9). The patient had been labeled by great psychiat-ric authorities as suffering from manic depressive insanity but Freud saw clearly that this was not so. (One of the greatest au-thorities, Professor Oswald Bumke, at that time in München, based his diagnosis on the fact that the patient sometimes was elated and sometimes deeply depressed when he came to him. Since he did not bother to find out whether there was anything in reality which could be responsible for these changes of mood, he could not find out the simple truth that the patient was in love with a nurse in the sanatorium where he was being treated and that whenever she responded to his love he was elated and whenever she did not he was depressed.) Freud saw that there was no manic depressive psychosis, merely a very rich, idle and bored young man. But he found something else; he found that the patient had been suffering from an infantile neurosis. The patient reported that before the age of four or five he developed a fear of wolves which was aroused largely by his sister who showed him again and again a picture book in which a wolf was represented. Whenever he saw this picture he began to scream and was afraid of the wolf coming and eating him up. Considering that he lived on a large estate in Russia, it is not unnatural that the little boy should have developed a fear of wolves, instigated by the threats of his sister. On the other hand he enjoyed beating horses. He also showed in this period signs of an obsessional neurosis, for instance by the obsession to think "God-Swine" or "God-Shit." And the patient suddenly called to mind that when he was still very small, less than five, his sister, two years older, who later committed suicide, seduced him into some kind of sexual play. Freud concluded that the little boy's sexual life "which was beginning to come under the sway of the genital zone, gave way before an external obstacle, and was thrown back by its influence into an earlier phase of pregenital organization" (Freud, 1918b, p. 25).

But all these data are relatively minor when compared to Freud's main interpretation, that of the Wolf Man's dream:

> I dreamt that it was night and that I was lying in my bed. (My bed stood with its foot toward the window; in front of the window there was a row of old walnut trees. I know it was winter when I had the dream, and nighttime.) Suddenly the window opened of its own accord, and I was terrified to see that some white wolves were sitting on the big walnut tree in front of the window. There were six or seven of them. The wolves were quite white, and looked more like foxes or sheep dogs, for they had big tails like foxes and they had their ears pricked like dogs when they pay attention to something. In great terror, evidently of being eaten up by the wolves, I screamed and woke up (p. 29f.).

What was Freud's interpretation of this dream?

The dream showed that the little boy had been sleeping in his cot at the age of one and a half years, woke up in the afternoon, possibly at five o'clock, and "witnessed a coitus *a tergo* [from behind] three times repeated; he was able to see his mother's genitals as well as his father's organ; and he understood the process as well as its significance. Lastly, he interrupted his parents' intercourse in a manner which will be discussed later" (p. 37-38).

Freud remarked:

"I have now reached the point at which I must abandon the support I have hitherto had from the course of the analysis. I am afraid it will also be the point at which the reader's belief will abandon me" (p. 36). Indeed, and more than that. To form a hypothesis about what actually happened when the boy was one and a half from a dream which says nothing more than that the boy saw some wolves, seems to be an example of obsessional thinking with complete disregard for reality. To be sure, Freud uses this association and weaves it together into a whole fabric but the fabric does not stand up with any claim to reality. This interpretation of the Wolf Man's dream, one of the classic examples of Freud's art of dream interpretation, is actually a testimony to Freud's capacity and inclination to build up reality out of a hundred little incidents either surmised or gained by interpretation, torn out of context and used in the service of arriving at certain conclusions that fit his preconceived idea.

Thus much can be said even if Freud arrives at what is an absurd interpretation: his capacity to observe and take into account even the smallest detail, in the dream as well as in the associations of the patient, is admirable. Nothing, small as it may be, seems to escape his attention; everything is reported with the greatest accuracy.

Unfortunately this has not remained true for many of his students. Lacking Freud's unusual power of penetrating thought and attention to detail, they have chosen an easier way and arrived at interpretations that are also absurd but are the result of some vague speculation which simplifies matters tremendously.

In fact, Freud never simplified, he complicated and overcomplicated to the point that, once in the middle of his interpretation, one almost feels in a labyrinth. Freud's method of thinking led one to discover that a phenomenon means what it seems to mean, but that it also may express its negation. He discovered that every emphasis on love could hide suppressed hate, that insecurity could be covered up by arrogance, fear by aggressiveness et cetera. This was an important discovery; however, it was also a dangerous one. The assumption that something means its opposite needs evidence and Freud was eager to find that evidence. If one is less careful, as many of his pupils were, one arrives very easily at hypotheses which are destructive of scientific thinking. In order not to be commonsensical and to show that one has a special knowledge, not a few psychoanalysts routinely assume that the patient was motivated by the opposite of what he thinks he is motivated by.

"Unconscious homosexuality" is one of the best examples. This is a part of Freudian theory by which quite a few people have been damaged. The analyst, to show that he looks beneath the surface, may suggest that the patient suffers from unconscious homosexuality. Assuming the patient has a very intense heterosexual life, it will be argued that this very intensity helps to repress an unconscious homosexuality. Or, assuming the patient has no sexual interest whatsoever in persons of his own sex, the argument will be that this complete absence of homosexual interest is a proof of the repression of homosexuality; that if a man praises the color of another man's tie, it is prima facie evidence of his unconscious homosexuality. The trouble of course is that with this method the absence of homosexuality can never be proven and not rarely analysis has continued for years in search of unconscious homosexuality for which there is no evidence at all except from the basic assumption that anything might mean the opposite of its overt meaning. This habit has had disastrous results because it permits a degree of arbitrariness in interpretation which often leads to completely erroneous conclusions. (There is a definite parallel between this vulgar Freudianism and the vulgar Marxism that is cultivated in Soviet theoretical thinking. Marx, like Freud, shows that something can mean its very opposite but for Marx too this was something one had to prove. In vulgar Marxist thought, however, this led to the conclusion that one can always claim that if something is not what it says, it is the opposite, and thus it is easy to manipulate thinking for one's own dogmatic purposes.)

2. The Greatness and Limitations of Freud's Discoveries

The goal of the following discussion is to show:

1. what Freud's greatest discoveries were;
2. how his philosophical and personal premises forced him to narrow down and to distort his discoveries;
3. how their significance is greatly enhanced if we free Freud's formulations from these distortions;
4. that this is equivalent to distinguishing what is essential and lasting and what is time-conditioned and socially contingent in Freud's theory.

This aim does not constitute a "revision" of Freud or "neo-Freudianism." It rather is a development of the essence of Freud's thought by critical interpretation of its philosophical basis, substituting historical for bourgeois materialism.

The Discovery of the Unconscious

To be sure, Freud was not the first to discover the phenomenon that we harbor thoughts and strivings which we are not aware of—that is to say, which are unconscious—and live a hidden life in our psyche. But Freud was the first to have made this discovery the center of his psychological system and he investigated unconscious phenomena in the greatest detail, with astonishing results. Basically Freud dealt with a discrepancy between thinking and being. We think one thing, for instance that our behavior is motivated by love, devotion, sense of duty, et cetera, and we are not aware that instead it is motivated by the wish for power, masochism, dependency. Freud's discovery was that what we think is not necessarily identical with what we are; that what a person thinks of himself may be, and usually is, quite different or even completely in contradiction to what he really is, that most of us live in a world of self-deception in which we take our thoughts as representing reality. In fact the historical importance of Freud's concept of the unconscious is that in a long tradition thinking and being were supposed to be identical and in the stricter forms of philosophical idealism only the thought (the idea, the word) was real, while the phenomenal world had no reality of its own.* Freud, by reducing a great deal of conscious thought to the role of a rationalization of drives, tended to destroy the foundations of the rationalism of which he was himself such an outstanding exponent. With his discovery of the discrepancy between thinking and being, Freud not only undermined the Western tradition of idealism in its philosophical and popular

---

*I want to say in passing that there seems to be a good deal of evidence that the belief in the superiority of the idea and the thought over material reality was a result of the victory of the patriarchal over the matriarchal system. Since men cannot create naturally, that is to say give birth in a natural way as women can, they insist that they can also give birth, not by their wombs but by their brains. See my interpretation of the myth of creation in *The Forgotten Language* (Fromm, 1951a).

forms, he also made a far-reaching discovery in the field of ethics. Until Freud, sincerity could be defined as saying what one believed. Since Freud this is no longer a sufficient definition. The difference between what I say and what I believe assumes a new dimension, namely that of my unconscious belief or my unconscious striving. If in pre-Freudian time a man was convinced that he punished his child because it helped the child's development he would have been quite honest, as long as he really believed that. After Freud the critical question has become whether his belief is not simply a rationalization of his sadistic wishes—that is to say, that he has pleasure in beating the child and only uses as a pretext the idea that such punishment is for the benefit of the child. In fact one might ethically prefer the one who is at least honest enough to admit his real motive; he would not only be more honest but less dangerous. There is no kind of cruelty and viciousness which has not been rationalized individually or in history as being motivated by good intentions. Since Freud, the sentence *I meant well* has lost its function as an excuse. Meaning well is one of the best rationalizations for acting badly, and nothing is easier than to persuade oneself of the validity of this rationalization.

There is a third result of Freud's discovery. In a culture like ours in which words play a tremendous role, the weight given to them often serves to neglect, if not to distort, experience. If somebody says "I love you" or "I love God" or "I love my country," he utters words which, in spite of the fact that he fully believes in their truth, may be utterly untrue and nothing but a rationalization of the person's wish for power, success, fame, money or an expression of his own dependence on his group. There might not be—and usually there is not—any element of love involved. Freud's discovery is not yet so generally accepted that people are instinctively critical of statements of good intentions or stories of exemplary behavior, nevertheless the fact is that Freud's theory is a critical theory, as Marx's was. Freud did not accept statements at face value; he looked at them skeptically even when he did not doubt the conscious sincerity of the person speaking. But conscious sincerity means relatively little within the whole of somebody's personality structure.

Freud's great discovery, with its fundamental philosophical and cultural consequences, was that of the conflict between thinking and being. But he restricted the importance of his discovery by assuming that essentially what is repressed is awareness of infantile sexual strivings and that the conflict between thinking and being is essentially that between thinking and infantile sexuality. This restriction is not surprising. As I said before, being under the influence of the materialism of his time, Freud sought the contents of that which was repressed in those strivings which not only were psychical and physiological at the same time, but also, which was obvious, were repressed in the society in which Freud lived—more specifically, in the middle class, with its Victorian morality, from which Freud and most of his patients came. He found proof that pathological phenomena—hysteria for instance—sometimes were expressions of repressed sexual strivings. What he did was to identify the social structure of his class and its problems with the problems inherent in human existence. This was indeed one of Freud's blind spots. For him, bourgeois society was identical with civilized society, and while he recognized the existence of peculiar cultures that were different from bourgeois society, they remained for him primitive, undeveloped.

Materialistic philosophy and the widespread repression of the awareness of sexual desires were the basis from which Freud constructed the contents of the unconscious. In addition he ignored the fact that very often sexual impulses do not owe their presence or intensity to the physiological substratum of sexuality, that on the contrary they are often the product of entirely different impulses which in themselves are not sexual. Thus a source of sexual desire can be one's narcissism, one's sadism, one's tendency to submit, plain boredom; and it is well known that power and wealth are important elements in arousing sexual desires.

Today, only two or three generations after Freud, it has become obvious that in the culture of the cities, sexuality is not the main object of repression. Since mass man is dedicated to becoming a *Homo consumens,* sex has become one of the main articles of consumption (and in fact one of the cheapest) creating the illusion of happiness and satisfaction. The conflicts to be observed in man, between conscious and unconscious strivings, are diverse. Here is a list of some of the more frequent of these conflicts:

consciousness of freedom—unconscious unfreedom
conscious good conscience—unconscious guilt feeling
conscious feeling of happiness—unconscious depression
conscious honesty—unconscious fraudulence
consciousness of individualism—unconscious suggestibility
consciousness of power—unconscious sense of powerlessness
consciousness of faith—unconscious cynicism and complete lack of faith
consciousness of loving—unconscious indifference or hate
consciousness of being active—unconscious psychic passivity and laziness
consciousness of being realistic—unconscious lack of realism

These are the true contradictions of today which are repressed and rationalized. They existed already during Freud's time but some of them not as drastically as they do now. But Freud paid no attention to them because he was fascinated by sex and its repression. In the development of orthodox Freudian psychoanalysis infantile sexuality still remains the cornerstone of the system. Analysis thus has served as a resistance against touching the real and most decisive conflicts within man and between men.

THE OEDIPUS COMPLEX

Another of the great discoveries of Freud is what is called the Oedipus complex, and he postulated that the unsolved Oedipus complex is at the bottom of every neurosis.

What Freud meant by the Oedipus complex is easily understood: The little boy, because of the awakening of his sexual strivings at an early age, say four or five years, develops an intense sexual attachment to and desire for his mother. He wants her, and the father becomes his rival. He develops hostility toward the father and wants to replace him and, in the last analysis, to do away with him. Feeling his father to be his rival the little boy is afraid of being castrated by the father-rival. Freud called this constellation the Oedipus complex because in the Greek myth it is Oedipus who falls in love with his mother without awareness that the beloved woman is his mother. When the incest is discovered he blinds himself, a symbol for castrating himself, and leaves his home and kin, accompanied only by his daughter Antigone.

Freud's great discovery here is the intensity of the attachment of the little boy to his mother or a mother figure. The degree of this attachment—of the wish to be loved and cared for by mother, not to lose her protection and, in many men, not to give up mother but rather to see her in women who, although the man's age, signify a mother for him—cannot be overestimated. This attachment exists in girls too but it seems to have a somewhat different outcome which has not been made clear by Freud, and which is indeed very difficult to understand.

The attachment of a man to his mother, however, is not difficult to understand. Even in intrauterine life she is his world. He is completely part of her, nourished by her, enveloped by her, protected by her and even after birth this situation does not change fundamentally. Without her help he would die, without her tenderness he would become mentally sick. She is the one who gives life and on whom his life depends. She can also take life away by refusing to fulfill her motherly functions. (The symbol of the mother's contradictory functions is the Indian goddess Kali, the creator of life and its destroyer.) The father's role in the first years of life is almost as negligible as his incidental function of procreating a child. While it is a scientific truth that the male sperm must unite with the female egg, it is an experiential truth that the man has practically no role whatsoever in the procreation of a child and the care for its life. Psychologically speaking, his presence is quite unnecessary and can be fulfilled equally well by artificial insemination. He may play a role again when the child reaches the age of four or five, as the one who teaches the child, who serves as an example, who is responsible for his intellectual and moral upbringing. Unfortunately he is often an example of exploitativeness, irrationality and immorality. He usually wants to mold his son in his own image so that he becomes useful to him in his work and becomes the heir to his possessions, and also to compensate him for his own failures by achieving what the father did not achieve.

The attachment to and dependence on the mother figure is more than an attachment to a person. It is a longing for a situation in which the child is protected and loved and has not yet any responsibility to bear. But it is not only the child who has that longing. If we say the child is helpless and hence needs the mother we must not forget that every human being is helpless in relation to the world as a whole. To be sure, he can defend himself and take care of himself up to a point, but considering the dangers, uncertainties, risks with which he is confronted, and on the other hand how little power he has to cope with physical illness, poverty, injustice, it seems open to question whether the adult is less helpless than the child. But the child has a mother who by her love wards off all dangers. The adult has—nobody. Indeed he may have friends, a wife, a certain amount of social security, yet even so the possibility of defending himself and of acquiring what he needs is very fragile. Is it surprising that he carries with him the dream of finding a mother again or of finding a world in which he can be a child again? The contradiction between the loving of the paradisiacal child existence and the necessities that follow from his adult existence can be rightly considered the nucleus of all neurotic developments.

Where Freud erred, and had to err because of his premises, was that he understood the attachment to mother as essentially one of a sexual nature. Employing his theory of infantile sexuality it was logical for him to assume that what binds a little boy to his mother is that she is the first woman in his life, close to him, and gives his sexual desires a natural object for which he has longed. This too is to a large extent true. There is ample evidence that the mother is for the little boy not only an object of affection but an object of sexual desire. But—and here is Freud's great error —it is not the sexual desire which makes the relationship to mother so intense and vital and the figure of the mother so important, not only in childhood but maybe for a person's entire life. Rather, this intensity is based on the need for the paradisiacal state I just spoke about.

Freud overlooked the well-known fact that sexual desires per se are not characterized by great stability. Even the most intense sexual relationship, if it is without affection and strong emotional ties, the most important being love, is rather short-lived and if one gives it six months one is probably being liberal. Sexuality as such is fickle and even more so perhaps in men, who are roving adventurers, than in women in whom the responsibility for a child gives sex a more serious meaning. To assume that men should be bound to their mothers because of the intensity of a sexual bond that had its origin twenty or thirty or fifty years earlier is nothing short of absurd considering that many are not bound to their wives after even three years of a sexually satisfactory marriage. Indeed, for little boys the mother may be an object of desire because she is one of the first women close to him, but it is also true, as Freud reports in his own case histories, that they are just as willing to fall in love with a little girl of their own age and have passionate love affairs with them, with mother relatively forgotten.

One does not understand the love life of a man if one does not see how it wavers between the wish to find the mother again in another woman, and the wish to get away from mother and to find a woman who is as different from the mother figure as any woman possibly could be. This conflict is one of the basic causes of divorce. It easily happens that the woman is not a mother figure when the marriage begins, but in married life, in which she takes care of the household, she often becomes a kind of disciplinarian who holds the man back from his childhood wish for new adventures; by this very fact, she assumes the function of the mother and as such is wanted by the man, and at the same time he is afraid of and repelled by her. Often an older man falls in love with a young girl, among other reasons because she is free from all motherly features and as long as she is infatuated with him the man has the illusion of having escaped his dependence on the mother figure. Freud in his discovery of the Oedipal tie to the mother uncovered one of the most significant phenomena, namely man's attachment to mother and his fear of losing her; he distorted this by explaining it as a sexual phenomenon and thus obscured the importance of his discovery that the longing for mother is one of the deepest emotional desires rooted in the very existence of man.

The other part of the Oedipus complex, the hostile rivalry with the father, culminating in the wish to kill him, is an equally valid observation which, however, has not necessarily anything to do with the attachment to mother. Freud gives a universal meaning to a feature that is characteristic only of patriarchal society. In a patriarchal society the son is subject to the father's will; he is owned by the father and his fate is determined by the father. In order to be the heir of the father—that is, broadly speaking, to be successful—he must not only please the father, he must submit to him, obey him and replace his own will with that of the father. As always, oppression leads to hate, to a wish to liberate oneself from the oppressor, and in the last analysis, to eliminate him. We see this situation clearly in examples such as the old peasant who rules like a dictator over his son, his wife, until the day he dies. If that day is far off, if the son reaches the age of thirty or forty or fifty and still has to accept the domination of his father, then indeed in many cases he will hate him as an oppressor. In the modern business world all this is greatly mitigated: the father does not usually own property to which the son would be heir, since the advancement of younger people is based to a large extent on their own capacities, and only rarely, as in personally owned enterprises, does the longevity of the father keep the son in an inferior position. Nevertheless, these are very recent developments and it is fair to say that through several thousand years of patriarchal society there was a built-in conflict between father and son based on the father's control over the son and the son's wish to rebel against it. Freud saw this conflict but did not recognize it for what it is, namely a feature of patriarchal society; instead he interpreted it as essentially the sexual rivalry between father and son.

Both observations, the nonsexual desire for protection and safety, the paradisiacal bliss, and the conflict between father and son as a necessary by-product of patriarchal society, were combined by Freud into a unit in which the attachment to mother was sexual and hence the father became a rival, a name to be feared and hated. The hatred toward the father because of sexual rivalry for mother has often been demonstrated by certain sayings of little boys, which are not infrequent: "When father dies I will marry you, Mommy." Such sayings are used as proof of the murderous impulses of the little boy and the extent of his rivalry with his father.

I do not believe they prove anything of the kind. Naturally the little boy has impulses during which he wants to be big like the father and to replace the father as a favorite of his mother. It is natural that in the between state in which all children over four live, of neither really being infants anymore nor being treated as adults, they have the wish to be big like adults; but the sentence *When father dies I shall marry you* is given undue weight by so many to mean that this little boy really wants his father to be dead. The little boy has no idea of what death is, and all he is really saying is "I wish father was away, so that I can get all her attention." To conclude that the son deeply hates the father, a hatred which includes this death wish, is to pay little attention to the world of imagination of the child and to the difference between him and the adult.

Let us have a look at the Oedipus myth in which Freud saw confirmed his construction of the tragic nature of the incestuous wishes of the little boy and the rivalry with the father (see also, regarding the following, Fromm, 1951a, chapter 7). Freud dealt only with the first of Sophocles' trilogy, *Oedipus Rex,* and this tragedy tells us that an oracle has told Laius, the King of Thebes, and his wife, Jocasta, that if they have a son this son will kill his father and marry his own mother. When a son, Oedipus, is born to them, Jocasta decides to escape the fate predicted by the oracle by having the infant killed. She gives Oedipus to a shepherd, who is to abandon the child in the woods with his feet bound so that he will die. But the shepherd, taking pity on the child, gives the infant to a man in the service of the King of Corinth, who in turn brings him to his master. The king adopts the boy, and the young prince grows up in Corinth not knowing that he is not the true son of the King of Corinth. He is told by the oracle in Delphi that it is his fate to kill his father and to marry his mother. He decides to avoid this fate by never going back to his parents. Leaving Delphi he engages in a violent argument with an old man riding in a carriage, loses his temper and slays the man and his servant without knowing that he has slain his father, the King of Thebes.

His wanderings lead him to Thebes. There the Sphinx is devouring the young men and women of the city, and she will cease doing so only if someone can find the right answer to a riddle she asks. The riddle is this: "What is it which first goes on four, then on two, and eventually on three?" The city of Thebes has promised that anyone who can solve the riddle and thus free the city from the Sphinx will be made king and will be given the king's widow for a wife. Oedipus undertakes the venture. He finds the answer—which is *man,* who as a child walks on four, as an adult on two, and in his old age on three (with a cane). The Sphinx throws herself into the ocean, the city is saved from calamity and Oedipus becomes king and marries Jocasta, his mother.

After Oedipus has reigned happily for some time, the city is ravaged by a plague which kills many of its citizens. The seer, Teiresias, reveals that the plague is the punishment for the two-fold crime which Oedipus has committed, patricide and incest. Oedipus, after having tried desperately not to recognize this truth, blinds himself when he is compelled to see it, and Jocasta commits suicide. The tragedy ends at the point where Oedipus has suffered punishment for a crime which he committed un-knowingly and in spite of his conscious effort to avoid committing it.

Was Freud justified in concluding that this myth confirms his view that unconscious incestuous drives and the resulting hate against the father-rival are to be found in every male child? Indeed, it does seem as if the myth confirms Freud's theory, and that the Oedipus complex justifiably bears its name.

If we examine the myth more closely, however, questions arise which cast some doubts on the correctness of this view. The most pertinent question is this: if Freud's interpretation is right, we should expect to be told that Oedipus meets Jocasta without knowing that she is his mother, falls in love with her and then kills his father, again unknowingly. But there is no indication whatso-ever that Oedipus is attracted by or falls in love with Jocasta. The only reason we are given for Oedipus' marriage to Jocasta is that she, as it were, goes with the throne. Should we believe that a story, the central theme of which constitutes an incestuous rela-tionship between mother and son, would entirely omit the ele-ment of attraction between the two? This question is all the more weighty in view of the fact that, in the older versions, only once does the oracle predict marriage to the mother, in the version by Nikolaus of Damascus, which according to Carl Robert is based on a relatively recent source (see Robert, 1915).

Considering this question we might formulate a hypothesis, namely that the myth can be understood as a symbol not of the incestuous love between mother and son but of the rebellion of the son against the authority of the father in the patriarchal family; that the marriage of Oedipus and Jocasta is only a secondary element, only one of the symbols of the victory of the son, who takes his father's place and with it all his privileges.

If we are thinking only of *Oedipus Rex* this hypothesis remains at best a hypothesis, but its validity can be decided by examining the whole Oedipus myth, particularly in the form presented by Sophocles in the two other parts of the trilogy, *Oedipus at Colonus* and *Antigone.* * This examination leads to a very different and new understanding of the material, at the center of which is the fight between patriarchal and matriarchal cultures.

In *Oedipus at Colonus* we find Oedipus exiled by Creon and accompanied by his daughters Antigone and Ismene, while his sons Eteocles and Polyneices refuse to help their blind father, whose throne they fight for. Eteocles wins but Polyneices, refusing to yield, seeks to conquer the city with outside help and to wrest power from his brother.

Thus far we have seen that one topic of the trilogy is the hate between father and son in a patriarchal society, but if we look at the trilogy as a whole we discover that Sophocles is speaking of the conflict between the patriarchal and the earlier matriarchal world. In the patriarchal world sons are fighting their fathers and fighting each other; the victor is Creon, the prototype of a Fascist

---

*While it is true that the trilogy was not written in this order and while some scholars may be right in their assumption that Sophocles did not plan the three tragedies as a trilogy, they must nevertheless be interpreted as a whole. It makes little sense to assume that Sophocles described the fate of Oedipus and his children in three tragedies without having in mind an inner coherence of the whole. (All Sophocles quotations are taken from Sophocles, 1955. Italics are added by E.F.)

ruler. Oedipus, however, is not accompanied by his sons but by his daughters. It is they on whom he relies while his relation to his sons is one of mutual hate. Historically, the original Oedipus myth, in the versons which existed in Greece and upon which Sophocles built his tragedy, gives an important clue. In these formulations, the figure of Oedipus is always connected with the cult of the earth goddesses, the representatives of matriarchal religion. In almost all versions of the myth, from parts which deal with the exposure of Oedipus as an infant to those which are centered around his death, traces of this connection can be found (see Schneidewin, 1852, p. 192). Thus, for instance, Eteonos, the only Boeotian city which had a cult shrine of Oedipus and where the whole myth probably originated, also had the shrine of the earth goddess Demeter (see Robert, 1915, p. 1 ff.). At Colonus (near Athens), where Oedipus finds his last resting place, was an old shrine of Demeter and the Erinyes which had probably existed prior to the Oedipus myth (Robert, p. 21). As we shall see, Sophocles has emphasized this connection between Oedipus and the chthonic goddesses in *Oedipus at Colonus.*

Oedipus' return to the grove of the goddesses, though the most important clue, is not the only one to the understanding of his position as representative of the matriarchal order. Sophocles makes another and very plain allusion to matriarchy by having Oedipus refer to Egyptian matriarchy when he tells about his daughters.* This is the way he praises them: "O true image of the *ways of Egypt that they show in their spirit and their life! For there the men sit weaving in the house, but the wives go forth to win the daily bread.* And in your case, my daughters, those to whom these toils belonged keep the house at home like girls, while ye, in their stead, bear your hapless father's burden."

The same trend of thought is continued by Oedipus when he compares his daughters to his sons. Of Antigone and Ismene he says: "Now, these girls preserve me, these my nurses, *these who are*

---

*Sophocles probably refers here to a passage from Herodotus, *History,* 2.35.

men not women, in true service: but ye are aliens, and no sons of mine."

In *Antigone* the conflict between the patriarchal and matriarchal principles finds its most radical expression. Creon, the ruthless authoritarian, has become the tyrant of Thebes, Oedipus' two sons have been killed, one while attacking the city to gain power, the other while defending it. Creon has ordered that the legitimate king should be buried and that the challenger's body should be left unburied, the greatest humiliation and dishonor to be done to a man, according to Greek custom. The principle that Creon represents is that of the supremacy of the law of the state over ties of blood, of obedience to authority over allegiance to the natural law of humanity. Antigone refuses to violate the laws of blood and of the solidarity of all human beings for the sake of an authoritarian, hierarchical principle. She stands for the freedom and happiness of the human being as against the arbitrariness of male rule. Therefore the Chorus can say, "Wonders are many, and none is more wonderful than man." In contrast to her sister Ismene who feels that women have to capitulate to the power of men, Antigone defies the principle of patriarchy. She follows the law of nature and equality and all-embracing motherly love and says, "It is not my nature to join in hating but in loving." Creon, his masculine superiority challenged, says, "Now verily I am no man, she is the man if this victory shall rest with her and bring no penalty," and turning to his son who has fallen in love with Antigone, he says, "Yea, this my son should be thy heart's fixed law—in all things to obey thy father's will." He continues, *"But disobedience is the worst of evils.* This it is that ruins cities; this makes home desolate; by this, the ranks of allies are broken into headlong rout; but, of the lives whose course is fair, the greater part owes safety to obedience. *Therefore we must support the cause of order, and in no wise suffer a woman to worst us. Better to fall from power, if we must, by a man's hand; than we should be called weaker than a woman."*

The conflict between Creon the patriarch and Haemon the

rebel against patriarchy and the defender of women's equality, comes to a climax when Haemon's answer to his father's question "Am I to rule the land by other judgement than my own?" is "That is no city which belongs to one man . . . Thou wouldst make a good monarch of a desert." Upon which Creon answers, "This boy, it seems, is the *woman's* champion." And Haemon points to the power of the matriarchal goddesses: "And for thee, and for me, and for the *gods below.*" (The gods below are the mother goddesses.) The conflict comes to its end. Creon has Antigone buried alive in a cave—again a symbolic expression of her connection with the goddesses of the earth. Stricken by panic, Creon tries to save Antigone but in vain. Haemon attempts to kill his father and when he fails, he takes his own life. Creon's wife, Eurydice, upon hearing the fate of her son, kills herself, cursing her husband as the murderer of her children. Creon has won physically. He has killed his son, the woman his son loved, and his wife, but morally he is indeed in bankruptcy, and admits it: "Ah me, this guilt can never be fixed on any other mortal kind, for my acquittal! I, even I, was thy slayer, wretched that I am— I own the truth. Lead me away, O my servants, lead me hence with all speed, whose life is but as death! . . . Lead me away, I pray you; a rash, foolish man; who have slain thee, ah, my son, unwittingly, and thee, too, my wife—unhappy that I am! I know not which way I should bend my gaze, or where I should seek support; for all is amiss with that which is in my hands;—and yonder again, a crushing fate hath leapt upon my head."

If we look now at the whole trilogy we must come to the conclusion that incest is not the main idea or even essential to the vision Sophocles expressed there. It may appear so if we read only *Oedipus Rex* (and how many people who speak glibly of the Oedipus complex have read the trilogy?), but considering the entire trilogy, Sophocles deals with the conflict between the matriarchal principle of equality and democracy represented by Oedipus, and the principle of patriarchal dictatorship of "law and order" represented by Creon. While patriarchy remains the victor in terms of power, its principles are morally defeated in the debacle of Creon who recognizes that he has achieved nothing but death.*

TRANSFERENCE

Another crucial concept in Freud's system is that of transference. This concept was the result of clinical observation. Freud found that analysands develop a very strong tie to the person of the analyst during the treatment, a tie which is in itself of a complex nature. It is a blend of love, admiration, attachment; in what is called "negative transference" it is a blend of hate, opposition and aggression. If the analyst and the analysand are of different sexes the essence of transference can be described easily as a case of the analysand's falling in love with the analyst (in the case of homosexual analysands the same would happen if the analyst was of the same sex). The analyst becomes the object of love, admiration, dependency and intense jealousy to the extent that anyone else is considered a possible rival. In other words, the analysand behaves exactly like a person who has fallen in love with the analyst. What makes this transference particularly interesting is that it grows out of the situation rather than the qualities of the analyst. No analyst can be so stupid or unattractive as not to produce this effect on an otherwise intelligent person who would not care to look at him if he was not his or her analyst.

While this transference can be found in relation to many physicians, Freud was the first to pay full attention to this phenomenon and to analyze its nature. He came to the conclusion that the analysand in the analytic process developed many feelings which he or she had as a child toward one of the parents. He explained the phenomenon of the loving (or hostile) attachment to the

---

*Sophocles protests against the denial of the older religious tradition which reached a climax in the teachings of the Sophists. In his arguments against the Sophists, he gave new expression to the old religious (matriarchal) traditions with emphasis on love, equality and justice.

figure of the analyst as a repetition of the earlier attachment to father or mother. In other words, the feelings toward the analyst were "transferred" from the original object to the person of the analyst. An analysis of transference made it possible, so Freud thought, to recognize—or reconstruct—what the attitude of the infant had been toward his or her parents. It was the child in the analysand who experienced his transferred feelings so intensely that it was often difficult for him to recognize that he did not love (or hate) the real person of the analyst but the parents whom the analyst represented for him.

This discovery was in itself one of Freud's great original findings. Until Freud nobody had cared to investigate the affective attitude of a patient toward the physician. Usually the physicians accepted with satisfaction that the patients "adored" them, and if they did not, often disliked them for not being "good patients." In fact transference is one factor conducive to the professional sickness of analysts, namely the confirmation of their narcissism by receiving the affectionate admiration of their analysands regardless of the degree to which they deserve it. It was Freud's genius to observe this phenomenon and not to interpret it as an expression of deserved admiration, but as a child's admiration for his parents.

The development of transference in the analytic situation was furthered by the peculiar arrangement which Freud chose for his work. The analysand lay on the couch, the analyst sat, invisible, behind him, listening most of the time and from time to time giving an interpretation. Freud once expressed his real motive for that arrangement, namely that he could not bear to be stared at by another person for many hours a day. As an additional reason, psychoanalysts mention that the analyst should be a blank piece of paper for the analysand so that all reactions to the analyst can be considered as expressions of transference rather than expressions of his feelings toward the real person of the analyst. The latter reasoning is of course an illusion. Just to look at a person, to sense the quality of his handshake, to hear his voice, to notice his whole attitude toward you when he is speaking, is plenty of material to enable you to know a lot about the analyst, and the idea that the analyst remains as unknown as he is invisible, is very naïve. A brief point of criticism of this technical arrangement may be in order. The entire constellation of the silent, allegedly unknown analyst who is not even supposed to answer a question, and his position of sitting behind the analysand (turning around and having a full look at the analyst is practically taboo)* actually results during the hour in the analysand's feeling like a little child. Where else is a grown-up person in such a position of complete passivity? All prerogatives are the analyst's and the analysand is obliged to utter his most intimate thoughts and feelings toward the phantom; this in terms not of a voluntary act but of a moral obligation that he accepts once he has agreed to be an analytic patient. From Freud's standpoint this infantilization of the analysand was all to the good since the main intention was to discover or reconstruct his early childhood,

One major criticism of this infantilization is that if the analysand is transformed into a child during the session, the adult person is, so to speak, removed from the picture and the analysand utters all his ideas and feelings that he had as a child, but he does not concern himself with the adult person in him, which has the capacity of relating to the child person from the standpoint of the adult. In other words he feels little of the conflict between his infantile and his adult self, and it is this very conflict that is conducive to improvement or change. When the voice of

*Some of my teachers at the Berlin Institute took short naps during the analysis and talked about it openly. Others claimed that during those naps they would have a dream about the analysand that gave them more insight than if they had listened. Of course, the tendency to snore was an obstacle to this practice and hence kept many from having the nap. These naps were only too natural. I know from my own experience during the years in which I analyzed according to the Freudian technique, how overwhelmingly tired I got in the position of sitting behind the analysand, having no contact with him or her and listening to the endlessly droning voice which I had no business to interrupt. In fact, it was this boredom which made the situation so unbearable that I began to change the technique.

the child is heard, who is there to contradict it, to answer to it, to restrain it, unless it is the voice of the adult that the analysand has also at his disposal? However, my main purpose in discussing transference is not an immanent critique from a therapeutic standpoint (which actually belongs to a discussion of psychoanalytic technique) but to show how Freud narrowed down his clinical experience of the transference by explaining that the feelings and attitudes characteristic of it are transferred from infantile life to the analytic situation.

If we discard this explanation we see that Freud hit on a phenomenon which is of much greater significance than even he thought. The transference phenomenon, namely the voluntary dependence of a person on other persons in authority, a situation in which an individual feels helpless, in need of a leader of stronger authority, ready to submit to this authority, is one of the most frequent and most important phenomena in social life, quite beyond the individual family and the analytic situation. Anybody who is willing to see can discover the tremendous role that transference plays socially, politically and in religious life. One has only to look at the faces in a crowd that applauds a charismatic leader like Hitler or de Gaulle, and one sees the same expression of blind awe, adoration, affection, something in fact which transforms the face from its humdrum daily expression into that of a passionate believer. It does not even have to be a leader with the voice or the stature of a de Gaulle or with the intensity of a Hitler. If one studies the faces of Americans who are looking at presidential candidates, or, a more obvious example, at the president himself, one finds the same particular facial expression, an expression that could almost be called religious. As in the psychoanalytic transference this has almost nothing to do with the real, human qualities of the admired person. The office itself or even simply a uniform makes him into a "worshipable" person.

Our whole social system rests upon this extraordinary effect of people who have appeal, to a greater or lesser degree. The transference in the analytic situation and the worship of leaders in adult life are not different: they have their basis in the sense of helplessness and powerlessness of the child which lead to its dependence on the parents, or in the transference situation on the analyst as a substitute for the parents. Indeed who could deny that the infant could not live for a day without being cared for, fed, protected by mother or her substitute? Whatever narcissistic illusions the child may have, the fact remains that with regard to its total situation in the world it is helpless and hence longing for a helper. What is often overlooked, however, is the fact that the adult is helpless too. In many situations which the child could not manage, the adult knows what to do but is, in the last analysis, also extremely helpless. He is confronted with natural and social forces which are so overwhelming that in many cases he is as helpless against them as the infant is in his world. True enough he has learned to defend himself in many ways. He can form ties with others, so as to be better equipped to withstand attacks and dangers, but all this does not alter the fact that he remains helpless in his fight against natural dangers, in the fight against better armed and more powerful social classes and nations, the fight against disease, and finally against death. He has better means of defense but is also much more aware of the dangers than the child is. It follows that the alleged contrast between the helpless child and the powerful adult is to a large extent fictitious.

The adult, like the child, is longing for somebody who would make him feel certain, secure, safe, and it is for that reason that he is willing and prone to worship figures that are, or readily lend themselves to being considered, saviors and helpers even if in reality they may be half mad. The social transference born out of the same sense of helplessness as the psychoanalytic transference is one of the most important social phenomena. Freud, in discovering transference in the psychoanalytic situation, made another universally valid discovery but on the basis of his premises could not fully appreciate the far-reaching social importance of what he had discovered.

This discussion of transference needs one additional remark. Even though man is helpless not only as a child but as an adult, this adult helplessness can be overcome. In a society which is rationally organized, which does not need to confuse man's mind in order to deceive him about the real situation, in a society that encourages rather than discourages man's independence and rationality, the sense of helplessness will have disappeared and with it the need for social transference. A society whose members are helpless needs idols. This need can only be overcome to the extent to which man is fully aware of reality and of his own forces. The insight that he must eventually die does not have to make him helpless because this knowledge too represents a piece of reality which he can cope with. Applying the same principle to the analytic situation I suggest that the more real the analyst is to the analysand and the more he loses his phantomlike character, the easier it is for the analysand to give up the posture of helplessness and to cope with reality. But is it not desirable and even necessary that the patient in the analytic situation regress to a state of childhood, so that he can express those desires and anxieties he is taught to repress as a condition of being accepted as an adult?

It is, but with an important qualification. If the analysand during the analytic hour becomes a child altogether, he might as well be dreaming. He would lack the judgment and independence which he needs in order to be able to understand the meaning of what he is saying. The analysand during the analytic session constantly oscillates between the infantile and the adult existence; on this very process rests the efficacy of the analytic procedure.

NARCISSISM

With the concept of narcissism Freud made a contribution of utmost importance for the understanding of man. Basically Freud postulated that man can orient himself in two contradictory modes: his main interest, love, concern—or as Freud puts it, his libido (sexual energy)—can either be directed toward himself or toward the world outside: people, ideas, nature, man-made things.

At a meeting of the Vienna Psycho-Analytical Society in 1909 Freud declared that narcissism was a necessary intermediate stage between autoeroticism and "object-love."* He did not look at narcissism primarily as a sexual perversion, the sexual love for one's own body, as had Paul Näcke, who introduced the term in 1899; rather, he saw it as a complement of the instinct of self-preservation.

The most important evidence of the existence of narcissism came from the analysis of schizophrenia. Schizophrenic patients were characterized by two features: megalomania and diversion of their interests from the external world—from people and things. The interest they had withdrawn from others they directed to their own person—and thus developed megalomania; the image of their own self as omniscient and omnipotent.

This concept of psychosis as a state of extreme narcissism was one basis of the idea of narcissism. The other was the normal development of the infant. Freud assumed that the infant exists in a completely narcissistic state, at the moment of birth, as it had been in the intrauterine state. Slowly the infant learns to take an interest in people and things. This original state of "libidinal cathexis of the ego" fundamentally persists and is related to the object-cathexis "much as the body of an amoeba is related to the pseudopodia which it puts out" (Freud, 1914c, p. 75).†

What was the importance of Freud's discovery of narcissism? It not only explained the nature of psychosis but it also showed that the same narcissism exists in the average adult as exists in

---

*The first full-fledged discussion of narcissism is to be found in *On Narcissism: An Introduction* (Freud, 1914c), where on p. 69 the editor traces the history of Freud's concept.
†Freud later revised some of the views represented here.

the child; to put it differently, that the "normal person" partakes to some lesser or greater degree in that attitude which, when quantitatively stronger, constitutes psychosis.

In what ways did Freud narrow down his concepts? Again, as with so many of his other concepts, by pressing it into the framework of the libido theory. Libido placed in the ego—occasionally sent out to touch other objects—returning to ego again under certain conditions such as physical pain, or the loss of a "libidinally cathected object." Narcissism was essentially a change of direction within the "libido household."

Had Freud not been the prisoner of the concept of the psychic "apparatus," an allegedly scientific version of human structure, he could have enhanced the significance of his discovery in many directions.

In the first place he might have emphasized more strongly than he did the role of narcissism in survival. While from a standpoint of values the maximal reduction of narcissism is desired, from the standpoint of biological survival narcissism is a normal and desirable phenomenon. If man did not put his own goals and needs before those of others, how could he survive? He would lack the energetic qualities of egoism necessary to take care of his own life. To put it differently: the biological interest of the survival of the race requires a certain amount of narcissism among its members; the ethico-religious goal of the individual, on the contrary, is the maximal reduction of narcissism toward the zero point.

But what is more important is Freud's failure to define narcissism in terms of its being the opposite pole of love. Freud could not have done so because, as I have shown before, love for him did not exist except as the attachment of the male to the feeding woman. For Freud, *to be loved* (the male by the conquered woman) gives strength, *to love actively* weakens.

This fact is very apparent in Freud's misunderstanding of Goethe in the *West-östlicher Divan*. Freud (1916–17, p. 418f.) writes: "You will find it refreshing, I believe, if, after what is the essen-

tially dry imagery of science, I present you with a poetic represen-
tation of the economic contrast between narcissism and being in
love. Here is a quotation from Goethe's *West-östlicher Divan:*

Zuleika

The slave, the lord of victories,
    The crowd, when'er you ask, confess
In sense of personal being lies
    A child of earth's chief happiness.

There's not a life we need refuse
    If our true self we do not miss,
There's not a thing we may not lose
    If one remain the man one is.

Hatem

So it is held, so well may be;
    But down a different track I come;
Of all the bliss earth holds for me
    I in Zuleika find the sum.

Does she expend her being on me,
    Myself grows to myself of cost;
Turns she away, then instantly
    I to my very self am lost.

That day with Hatem all were over;
    And yet I should but change my state;
Swift, should she grace some happy lover,
    In him I were incorporate.

Goethe's picture of one who remains "the man one is" is mis-
understood to portray the narcissistic person, while for Goethe,
of course, he is the mature independent man of integrity. The
second verse is supposed by Freud to represent the person who
lacks a strong self and is dissolved in the person he is in love with.

While according to Freud a man's love is "anaclitic," i.e., it has
as its object the person who feeds him, Freud assumes that

women's love is narcissistic, that they only can love themselves, and cannot participate in that great "achievement" of men: to love the hand that feeds them. Freud is unaware that the women of his class were cold precisely because their men wanted them cold, i.e., to behave like property, and not even to grant them "separate but equal" roles in bed. The bourgeois man got the woman as he imagined her and he rationalized his superiority by believing this deformed female—deformed by him—was only concerned with wanting to be fed and taken care of. This is of course typical male propaganda in the war between the sexes, another example of which is that women are less realistic and less courageous than men. Indeed, this insane world which does not seem to stop running into catastrophe is governed by men. As to courage, everybody knows that in cases of illness women are much better able to cope with difficulties than men, who want mother to help them. As to narcissism, women are forced to present themselves attractively, because they are exhibits on the slave market; but when they love they love more deeply and reliably than men, who roam around and try to satisfy their narcissism, invested in their penises of which they are so proud.

When Freud presented his distorted picture of women, he could not help considering whether he was entirely objective. But he did away with such doubts in an elegant way: "Perhaps it is not out of place here to give an assurance that this description of the feminine form of erotic life is not due to any tendentious desire on my part to depreciate women. Apart from the fact that tendentiousness is quite alien to me, I know that these different lines of development correspond to the differentiation of functions in a highly complicated biological whole; further, I am ready to admit that there are quite a number of women who love according to the masculine type and who also develop the sexual overvaluation proper to that type" (Freud, 1914c, p. 89).

This indeed is an elegant but not a psychoanalytic way out. What self-delusion in a man when he can assure us that "tendentiousness is quite alien to me" even in a question which is so obviously charged with emotional dynamite.*

This physiological concept of libido cathexes of ego as against objects has made it somewhat difficult, for those who are not among the initiated ones, to understand the nature of narcissism on the basis of their own experience. For this reason I want to describe it in a more easily understandable manner.

To narcissistic persons the only sector that seems fully real is their own person. Feeling, thoughts, ambitions, wishes, body, family, everything that they are or what is theirs. What they think is true, because they think it, and even their bad qualities are beautiful because they are theirs. Everything related to them has color and full reality. Everybody and everything outside is gray, ugly, without color, hardly existing.

Here is an example: A man called me to ask for an appointment. I answered that I had no free time in the week but could see him during the following week. He responded by pointing out that he lived very near to my office and hence it would take him little time to come over. When I answered that this was indeed convenient for him but it did not alter the fact that *I* had no free time, he was unimpressed and continued with the same argument. This is an example of a rather severe case of narcissism, because he was totally unable to distinguish between my needs and his.

It is obvious that it makes a great difference how intelligent, artistically talented, knowledgeable a very narcissistic person is. Many artists and creative writers, music conductors, dancers and politicians are extremely narcissistic. Their narcissism does not interfere with their art; on the contrary it often helps. They have to express what they subjectively feel, and the more important their subjectivity is to their performance, the better they perform.

---

*This statement points to the limitations of Freud; insight into himself is narrowed down by various dogmatic statements about personality traits which he "obviously" cannot possess!

The narcissistic person is often particularly attractive for his or her very narcissism. Think for example of a narcissistic entertainer. He is filled with himself; he exhibits his body and his wit with the pride of owning a rare jewel. He has no doubts about himself as a less narcissistic person necessarily has. What he says, does, the way he walks and moves is enjoyed by himself like a precious performance and he himself is one of his greatest admirers.

I assume that the reason for the attractiveness of the narcissistic person lies in the fact that he portrays an image of what the average person would like to be: he is sure of himself, has no doubts, feels always on top of the situation. The average person, in contrast, does not have this certainty; he is often plagued by doubts, prone to admire others as being superior to himself. One may ask why extreme narcissism does not repel people. Why do they not resent the lack of real love? This question is easy to answer: real love is so rare today as to be almost outside the field of vision of most people. In the narcissist one sees someone who at least loves *one* person, himself.

The completely untalented narcissist, on the other hand, may be only ridiculous. If the narcissistic person is extremely gifted, his success is virtually guaranteed. Narcissistic people are often to be found among successful politicians. Even if they are talented or gifted they would not be so impressive without the narcissism that, as it were, oozes out of them. Instead of feeling "How do they dare to be so arrogant?" many people are so attracted by the narcissistic self-image projected that they see in it nothing more than the adequate self-appreciation of a very talented man.

It is important to understand that narcissism, which may be called "self-infatuation," is in contrast to love, if we mean by love the act of forgetting oneself and caring more for others than for oneself.

Of equal importance is the contradiction between narcissism and reason. Since I have just talked about politicians as examples of narcissistic personalities, a statement about the conflict between narcissism and reason seems absurd. However, I am not speaking of intelligence but of reason. Manipulative intelligence is the capacity to use thinking for manipulating the world outside for man's purposes. Reason is the faculty to recognize things as they are, regardless of their value or danger to us. Reason aims at the recognition of things and persons in their suchness, undistorted by our subjective interest in them. Cleverness is a form of manipulating intelligence, but wisdom is an outcome of reason. The narcissistic person can be extremely clever, if his manipulative intelligence is at its best. But he is apt to make severe mistakes, because his narcissism seduces him into overestimating the value of his own wishes and thoughts and into assuming that the result has already been accomplished, simply because it is *his* wish or *his* thought.

Narcissism is often confused with egoism. Freud thought that narcissism was the libidinous aspect of egoism—that is to say, that the passionate nature of egoism lay in its libidinous character. But the distinction is not entirely satisfactory. An egoistic person may have an undistorted view of the world. He may not give to *his* thoughts and feelings a greater value than they have in the outside world. He may see the world, including his role in it, quite objectively. Egoism is basically a form of greediness; the egoist wants everything for himself, he does not like to share, he perceives others as threats rather than as possible friends. What Freud in his earlier writings called "self-interest" prevails in them more or less completely; but the prevalence of self-interest does not necessarily distort the egoist's picture of himself and the world around him, as it does with the narcissistic person.

Among all character orientations narcissism is by far the most difficult to recognize in oneself. To the extent to which a person is narcissistic he glorifies himself and is unable to see his defects and limitations. He is convinced that the image he has of himself as a wonderful person is correct, and since it is *his* image he sees no reason to doubt it. Another reason why narcissism is so difficult to detect in oneself is that many narcissistic persons try to demonstrate that they are anything but narcissistic. One of the most frequent examples of this is the attempt of narcissistic persons to hide their narcissism behind a behavior which is characterized by concern and help for others. They spend much energy and time in helping others, even making sacrifices, being kind, et cetera, all with the aim (usually unconscious) of denying this narcissism. The same goes, as we all know, for persons who are particularly modest or humble. Not only do such people often try to hide their narcissism, they satisfy it at the same time by being narcissistically proud of their kindness or modesty. A nice example of this is the joke about a dying man overhearing his friends who were at his bedside praise him—how learned he was, how intelligent, how kind, how concerned. The dying man listened and when they had finished praising he angrily shouted, "And you failed to mention my humility!"

Narcissism wears many masks: saintliness, obedience to duty, kindness and love, humility, pride. It ranges from the attitude of a haughty and arrogant person to that of a modest and unobtrusive one. Everybody has many tricks to disguise his or her narcissism and is hardly aware of them and their function. If the narcissistic person is successful in persuading others to admire him, he is happy and functions well. But when he is without success in convincing others, if his narcissism is pricked, as it were, he may collapse like a deflated balloon; or he may be intensely furious, filled with unforgiving rage. To inflict a wound on a person's narcissism may either produce a depression or an unforgiving hate.

Of particular interest is group narcissism. Group narcissism is a phenomenon of the greatest political significance. After all, the average person lives in social circumstances which restrict the development of intense narcissism. What should feed the narcissism of a poor man, who has little social prestige, whose children even tend to look down upon him? He is nothing—but if he can identify with his nation, or can transfer his personal narcissism to the nation, then he is everything. If such a person said, "I am the most wonderful man or woman in the world; I am the cleanest, cleverest, most efficient, best educated of all people; I am superior to everybody in the world," anybody who heard this would be disgusted and feel that the person was a bit crazy. But when people describe their nation in these terms, nobody takes exception. On the contrary, if a person says, "My nation is the strongest, the most cultured, the most peace-loving, the most talented of all nations," he is not looked upon as being crazy but as a very patriotic citizen. The same holds true for religious narcissism. That millions of adherents to a religion can claim that they are the only possessors of the truth, that their religion is the only way to salvation, is considered to be perfectly normal. Other examples of group narcissism are political groups and scientific groups. The individual satisfies his own narcissism by belonging to and identifying himself with the group. Not he the nobody is great, but he the member of the most wonderful group on earth.

But, so one might object, how can we be sure that his evaluation of his group is not realistically correct? For one thing, a group can hardly be as perfect as its members describe it; the more important reason, though, is that criticism of the group is responded to with intense rage, which is the reaction characteristic of one whose individual narcissism is wounded. In the narcissistic character of national, political and religious group reaction lies the root of all fanaticism. When the group becomes the embodiment of one's own narcissism, any criticism of the group is felt to be an attack against oneself.

In cases of cold or hot wars, the narcissism takes on a still more drastic form. My own nation is perfect, peace-loving, cultured, et cetera; the enemy's is the contrary—vile, treacherous, cruel, et cetera. In reality most nations are equal in the overall balance of good and evil traits; however, virtues and vices are specific for each nation. What narcissistic nationalism does is to see only the virtues of one's own and the vices of the enemy's nation. The mobilization of group narcissism is one of the important conditions for the preparation of war; it must begin much earlier than at the outbreak of the war, but it becomes reinforced the closer nations move toward war. The feelings at the beginning of the First World War are a good example of reason's becoming silenced when narcissism rules. British war propaganda accused the German soldiers of bayoneting infants in Belgium (a complete lie but believed by many in the West); the Germans called the British a nation of treacherous traders while they themselves were heroes fighting for freedom and justice.

Can this group narcissism ever disappear and with it one condition for war? Indeed there is no reason to assume that it cannot. The conditions for its disappearance are manifold. One is that the life of individuals must be so rich and interesting that they can relate to others with interest and love. This in turn presupposes a social structure that engenders being and sharing and discourages having and possessing (see Fromm, 1976a). With the development of interest in and love for others, narcissism tends to be increasingly reduced. The most important and most difficult problem, however, is that group narcissism can be produced by the basic structure of society, and the question is how this happens. I shall try to sketch an answer by analyzing the relation between the structure of industrial cybernetic society and the narcissistic development of the individual.

The first condition for the increasing development of narcissism in industrial society is the separateness and antagonism of individuals toward each other. This antagonism is a necessary consequence of an economic system that is built on ruthless selfishness and on the principle of seeking advantages at the expense of others. When sharing and mutuality are absent narcissism is bound to thrive. But the more important condition for the development of narcissism, and one which has been given full measure only in the last decades, is the worship of industrial production. Man has made himself into a god. He has created a new world, the world of man-made things, using the old creation only as raw material. Modern man has laid bare the secrets of the microcosmos as well as the macrocosmos; he has discovered the secrets of the atom and the secrets of the cosmos, relegating our earth to an infinitely small entity among the galaxies. The scientist making these discoveries had to perceive things as they are, objectively and hence with little narcissism. But the consumer, in the same way as the technicians and practitioners of applied science, has not had to have the mind of a scientist. The overwhelming part of the human race has not had to devise the new technics; they have been able to build it according to the new theoretical insights and admire it. Thus it happens that modern man has developed an extraordinary pride in his creation; he has deemed himself to be a god, he has felt his greatness in the contemplation of the grandeur of the man-made new earth. Thus admiring his second creation, he has admired himself in it. The world he has made, harnessing the energy of coal, of oil, and now of the atom, and especially the seeming limitless capacity of his brain, has become the mirror in which he can see himself. Man gazes into this mirror which reflects not his beauty but his ingenuity and power. Will he drown in this mirror as Narcissus drowned gazing at the picture of his beautiful body mirrored in the lake?

CHARACTER

Freud's concept of character is of no less importance than that of the unconscious, of repression and resistance. Here Freud dealt with the human being as a whole and not only with single "complexes" and mechanisms, such as the "Oedipus complex," castration fear, penis envy. Of course, the concept of character was not new; but the concept of character in the dynamic sense in which Freud used it was new in psychology. What is meant by dynamic here is the concept of character as the *relatively permanent structure of passions.* Psychologists during Freud's time spoke of character in a purely descriptive sense, as many still do today; a person could have been described as orderly, ambitious, industrious, honest, et cetera, but one would have been referring to single *traits* to be found in a person, not to the organized system of passions. Only the great playwrights such as Shakespeare, and the great novelists such as Dostoevski and Balzac, described character in the dynamic sense, the latter with the intention of analyzing the character of the various classes of French society of his time.

Freud was the first to analyze character scientifically instead of artistically as his novelist-predecessors had done. The results, enriched by some of Freud's students, especially K. Abraham, were marvelous. Freud and his school constructed four types of character structure: the oral-receptive character, the oral-sadistic character, the anal-sadistic character and the genital character. According to Freud, each person who develops in a normal way passes through all these stages of character structure; but many are stuck at any one of these points of evolution and retain as adults the features of these preadult character stages.

By the oral-receptive character Freud means the person who expects to be fed, materially, emotionally and intellectually. He is the person with the "open mouth," basically passive and dependent, who expects that what he needs will be given to him, either because he or she deserves it for being so good, or so obedient, or because of a highly developed narcissism that makes a person feel he is so wonderful that he can claim to be taken care of by others. This type of person expects that all satisfactions will be offered to him without any reciprocity.

The oral-sadistic person also believes that everything he needs comes from the outside and not from his own work. But unlike the oral-receptive character he does not expect anyone to give him what he needs voluntarily, but tries to take what he needs from others by force; his is a predatory exploitative character.

The third type of character is the anal-sadistic one. This is the character structure of persons who do not feel that anything new is ever created; that the only way to have something is to save what they have. They consider themselves as a kind of fortress, which nothing may leave. Their safety lies in isolation. Freud found in them the three following characteristics: to be orderly, parsimonious and obstinate.

The fully developed and, as it were, mature character is the genital character. While the three "neurotic" character orientations can be clearly recognized, the genital character is very vague. Freud describes it as being the basis for the capacity to love and to work. After what we have seen about Freud's concept of love, we know that he can refer only to the degraded form of love in a society of profit makers. What Freud means by the genital character is simply the bourgeois man—that is, the man whose capacity for love is very restricted and whose "work" is the effort of organizing and using the work of others, to be the manager and not the worker.

The three "neurotic" or as Freud would put it "pregenital" character orientations are a key to the understanding of human character exactly because they do not refer to a single *trait* but to the whole character *system.* It is in general easy to recognize to which type of character a person belongs even if one has only a few clues. The tight-lipped, withdrawn man whose first concern is that everything must be orderly and right, who shows little spontaneity, whose skin color tends to be sallow, is easily recognizable as an anal character; if one knows that he tends to be stingy, ungiving, distant, one receives confirmation. The same holds true for the exploitative and the receptive character types. It is true of course that a person tries to hide his true face, provided he is aware of the fact that it betrays trends that he would rather not divulge. Hence facial expressions are not even the most important indications of character structure. More important are those expressions that are much less controllable: the movements, the voice, the gait, the gestures and all that of a person which is in our field of vision when we look at him or see him walking.

People who have understood the meaning of the three pregenital character traits can without difficulty understand each other when they speak of this or that person as an anal character or when they speak of a mixture of anal/oral traits or especially oral-sadistic traits. It was Freud's genius to have captured in these character orientations all the possible ways in which man can relate himself to the world in the "process of assimilation" —that is to say, in the process of getting from nature or from other human beings what is necessary for survival. The problem is not that we all need to get something from the outside; even the saint could not survive without any food. The real problem is what our method of getting it is, whether it is a method of being given, robbing, hoarding or producing.

Since Freud and some of his pupils presented this characterology, our understanding of man and of cultures has been greatly enhanced. I say of cultures because societies can be characterized also in terms of these structures because their respective social characters—that is to say, the core of character common to most members of a society—will also be of the one or the other type. Just to give an example: the character of the French middle class of the nineteenth century was that of the anal character structure, the character of the entrepreneur of the same period, that of the exploiter.

The foundations of characterology that Freud laid led to the discovery of other forms of character orientations. One can speak of an authoritarian versus egalitarian character, of a destructive versus loving character, and in this way refer to an outstanding trait which determines the rest of the character structure.

The study of character has hardly begun and the consequences of Freud's discovery are far from exhausted. But all this admiration for Freud's theory of character must not prevent one from seeing that he narrowed down the significance of the theory by linking it up with sexuality. He had expressed that very clearly already in the *Three Essays on the Theory of Sexuality*: "What we call the *character* of the person is built up to a large extent from the material of sexual excitations; it is composed of impulses fixed since infancy and won through sublimation, and of such struc-

tures as are destined to suppress effectually those perverse feelings which are recognized as useless" (Freud, 1905d, p. 233f.
Italics by E.F.). His naming of the character orientations makes
this very clear. The two first receive their energy from oral libido,
the third from anal libido and the fourth from the so-called genital libido—that is to say, the sexuality in the adult man or woman.
The most important contribution of Freud to his characterology
is the paper *Character and Anal Erotism* (Freud, 1908b). All three
traits of the anal character—orderliness, parsimoniousness and
obstinacy—are seen as direct expressions of, reaction formation
to or sublimation of, anal libido. The same holds true for the
other character structures in terms of the oral and genital libido.

Freud subsumed many of the great passions such as love, hate,
ambition, thirst for power, avarice, cruelty, as well as the passion
for independence and freedom, under the various kinds of libido.
Love and hate in the newer part of Freud's theories concerning
the death and life instincts were supposed to have an essentially
biological origin. For the construction of the theory of life and
death instincts orthodox analysts have assumed that aggression
is as original an impulse inherent in human nature as love is. The
wish for power has been dealt with in connection with the anal-
sadistic character, although it must be admitted that the wish for
power, perhaps the most important impulse to be found in modern man, has not found adequate consideration in psychoanalytic
literature. Dependency has been dealt with in terms of submis-
sion as related to the Oedipus complex in various ways. (This
reduction of the great passions to various kinds of the libido was
a theoretical necessity for Freud, since aside from man's striving
for survival,* all energies within him were supposed to be of a
sexual nature.)

If one is not under a compulsion to explain all human passions

---

*In his later theory of death instinct and life instinct Freud replaced the older
essentially physiologically oriented theory with a biological theory of the polarity
between integrating forces–life instinct and destructive forces–death instinct (see
the discussion of Freud's theory of instincts in chapter 4).

as being rooted in sexuality, one is not forced to accept the Freudian explanation; one arrives at a simpler and, I believe, more accurate analysis of human passions. One can distinguish between biologically given passions, hunger and sex, which serve the survival of the individual and the race, and passions which are socially and historically conditioned. Whether people predominantly love or hate, submit or fight for freedom, are stingy or magnanimous, are cruel or tender, depends on the social structure that is responsible for the formation of all passions except the biological ones (see Fromm, 1968h). There are cultures in which, in their social character, the passion for cooperation and harmony dominates—for instance, the Zuni Indians of North America—and others in which extreme possessiveness and destructiveness dominate, as with the Dobu (see the detailed discussion of societies with either aggressive or sharing attitudes in Fromm, 1973a, chapter 8). Detailed analysis of the social character typical of any given society is required in order to understand how economic, geographical, historical and genetic conditions have led to the formation of various types of social character. To give a simple example: A tribe which has too little fertile soil, and even lacks supplies of fish and animals, is likely to develop a belligerent, aggressive character because its only way of survival is by robbing and stealing from other tribes. On the other hand, a tribe that does not produce a great surplus but enough for all to live, will tend to develop a peaceful and cooperative spirit. This example is of course oversimplified; the problem of which conditions cause a certain type of social character to develop is a difficult one and requires thorough analysis of all relevant and even seemingly irrelevant factors. This is the field of social analysis or historical analysis, which I believe has a great future, although until now only the foundations of this branch of analytic social psychology have been laid.

The historically conditioned passions are of such intensity that they can be greater than even the biologically conditioned passions of survival, hunger, thirst and sex. This may not be so for the average person whose passions have been largely reduced to the satisfaction of his physiological needs, but it is so for a considerable number of people in any historical period who risk their lives for their honor, their love, their dignity—or their hate. The Bible expressed that in simple words: "Man shall not live by bread alone" (Matt. 4:4). Let us imagine that Shakespeare had written his dramas about the sexual frustration of a hero or about a heroine's wish for food; they would have been as banal as some of the contemporary plays which are produced on Broadway. The dramatic element in human life is rooted in nonbiological passions and not in hunger and sex. Hardly anybody commits suicide because of the frustration of his or her sexual desires, but many are ready to give up living because their ambition or their hate has been frustrated.*

Freud never saw the individual as an isolated being, but always in his or her relationship to others. As he wrote: "Individual psychology, to be sure, is concerned with the individual human being, and it examines the ways in which he tries to satisfy his instinctual drives. But only rarely and under specific exceptional circumstances is it in a position to abstract from this person's relationships with other individuals. In the individual's psychic life, other people usually must be considered as either models, objects, helpers or opponents. Thus, from the beginning, individual psychology is simultaneously social psychology—in this extended but legitimate sense" (Freud, 1921c, p. 65). Nevertheless, this nucleus of a social psychology did not develop further because the ultimate entity for Freud, family life, was supposed to be decisive to the child's development. Freud did not see that the human being, from early childhood on, lives in several circles; the narrowest one is the family, the next one is his class, the third one is the society in which he lives, the fourth one the biological conditions of being human in which he participates, and finally,

---

*It is an interesting fact that the suicide rate by and large has risen in the same proportion as the rate of industrialization (see Fromm, 1955a, chapter 1).

he is part of a larger circle of which we know almost nothing, but which comprises at least our solar system. Only the narrowest circle, that of the family, had relevance for Freud, and thereby he greatly underestimated all other circles of which man is part. More specifically, he did not recognize that the family itself is determined by the class and social structure and constitutes an "agency of society" whose function it is to transmit the character of society to the infant even before it has any direct contact with society. This is done through early upbringing and education, as well as through the character of the parents which is in itself a social product (see Fromm, 1932a).

Freud considered the bourgeois family as the prototype of all families and ignored the very different forms of family structure and even the complete absence of the "family" in other cultures. An example of this is the great significance that Freud gives to the so-called "primal scene" in which the child witnesses the sexual intercourse of the parents. It is obvious that the significance of this experience is inflated by the fact that in the bourgeois family children and parents live in different rooms. Had Freud thought of the family life among the poorer classes of his time, where children lived in the same room with their parents and were witnesses to their intercourse routinely, this early experience would not have seemed so important to Freud. He also did not consider the many so-called primitive societies in which there was no taboo on sexuality and neither the parents nor the children had to hide their sexual acts and plays.

From the premises Freud held concerning all passions being of a sexual nature and of the bourgeois family being the prototype of all families, he could not see that the primary phenomenon is not the family but the structure of society that creates the kind of character it needs for its proper functioning and survival. He did not arrive at the concept of a "social character" because on the narrow basis of sex, such a concept could not be developed. As I have shown (Fromm, 1941a, appendix), the social character is that character structure which is common to most members of a society; its contents depend on the necessities of a given society which mold the character of the individual in such a way *that people want to do what they have to do* in order to secure the proper functioning of society. What they want to do depends on the dominating passions in their character, which have been formed by the necessities and requirements of a specific social system. The differences brought about by diverse family constellations is minor in comparison with the differentiation brought about by different structures of society and present in the respective classes. A member of the feudal class had to develop a character which enabled him to rule others, to harden his heart toward their misery. The bourgeois class of the nineteenth century had to develop an anal character which was determined by the wish to save and to hoard and not to spend. In the twentieth century the same class developed a character which made saving only a minor virtue, if not a vice, when compared with the trait of the modern character to spend and to consume. This development is conditioned by fundamental economic necessities: in the period of primary accumulation of capital, saving was necessary; in a period of mass production, instead of saving, spending is of the greatest economic importance. If the character of twentieth-century man suddenly reverted to that of nineteenth-century man, our economy would be confronted with a severe crisis, if not collapse.* Thus far I have described in oversimplified terms the problem of the relationship between individuals and social psychology. A fuller analysis of this problem, which would go beyond the limits of this book, would have to distinguish between needs or passions rooted in the existence of human beings and those that are not primarily conditioned by society but by the very nature of man, the absence of which must be considered as the

---

*My own studies of the social character continue the line of research which was begun by Sombart, Max Weber, L. J. Brentano, Tawney, Kraus and other social scientists in the first part of this century and I have greatly benefited from their theories.

result of repression or of severe social pathology. Such strivings are those for freedom, for solidarity, for love.

If Freud's system is freed from the narrowing effect of his libido theory, the concept of character has even greater importance than Freud himself gave to it. This requires the transformation of individual psychology into social psychology and reduces individual psychology only to the knowledge of small variations brought about by individual and idiosyncratic circumstances which influence the basic socially determined character structure. In spite of this critique of Freud's concept of character, it must be emphasized again that Freud's discovery of the dynamic concept of character offers the key to the understanding of the motivation of individual and social behavior and to some extent, the prediction of it.

THE SIGNIFICANCE OF CHILDHOOD

Among the great discoveries of Freud is that of the significance of early childhood. This discovery has several aspects. The infant has already sexual (libidinous) strivings, although not yet in terms of genital sexuality but in what Freud terms "pregenital sexuality," which is centered on the "erogenous zones" of mouth, anus and skin. Freud recognized the fictitiousness of the bourgeois picture of the "innocent" child and showed that from birth on the little child is endowed with many libidinous strivings of a pregenital nature.

At Freud's time the myth of the innocent child who knows nothing of sex still governed;* furthermore one was not aware of what importance the experiences of the child and particularly the

---

*It must be noted that the whole concept of a child as having a special status in contrast with that of the adult is relatively modern. Until the eighteenth century this division hardly existed, the child was simply a small adult who was not romanticized and did his chores according to his abilities. I am grateful to Ivan Illich for some fruitful suggestions in this direction.

very young child had for the development of his character and thereby of his whole fate. With Freud all this changed. He could show by many clinical examples how early events, especially those of a traumatic nature, formed the character of the child to such a degree that Freud could assume that, with rare exceptions, long before puberty the character of a person was fixed and did not undergo further changes. Freud showed how much a child knew, how sensitive it was, how events which may sound trifling to an adult deeply influenced the development of the child and later formation of neurotic symptoms. For the first time one began to take the child and what happened to him seriously, so seriously indeed that one believed one had found the key to all further development in the events of early childhood. A great deal of clinical data show the correctness and wisdom of Freud's observation, but I believe they also show certain limitations in his theoretical assumptions.

In the first place Freud underrated the significance of constitutional, genetic factors in the character formation of children. He did not do so in theory, stating that constitutional factors and experience are both responsible for the development of the person, but for all practical purposes he and most psychoanalysts neglected the genetic disposition of a person; in crude Freudianism it is exclusively the family and the experience of the child in it which are made responsible for the development of the child. This has gone so far that psychoanalysts as well as parents believe that a neurotic or bad or unhappy child must have parents who have produced this negative state, while on the contrary the happy and healthy child has a correspondingly happy and healthy environment. In fact parents have taken the whole of the blame for the unhealthy development of a child on themselves and equally so the praise for the happy outcome of childhood. All data show that they should not have done so. Here is a good example: A psychoanalyst may see a very neurotic, distorted person with a terrible childhood and say, "It is obvious that the childhood experiences have produced this unhappy outcome." If he would only ask himself, however, how many people he had seen who came from the same type of family constellation and turned out to be remarkably happy and healthy people, he would begin to have doubts about the simple connection between childhood experiences and the mental health or illness of a person.

The first factor which accounts for this theoretical disappointment must lie in the analyst's ignoring the differences in genetic dispositions. To take a simple example: One can see even among newborn infants a difference in degree of aggressiveness or timidity. If the aggressive child has an aggressive mother, this mother will do him little harm or perhaps even much good. It will learn to fight with her and not be frightened of her aggressiveness. If a timid child is confronted with the same mother, it will be intimidated by the mother's aggressiveness, it will tend to become a frightened, submissive and later on perhaps a neurotic person.

Indeed, we touch here upon the old and much discussed problem of "nature versus nurture" or genetic disposition versus environment. The discussion of this problem has by no means yet led to conclusive results. From my own experience I have come to the conclusion that genetic dispositions play a much greater role in the formation of a specific character than most analysts credit it with doing. I believe that one aim of the analyst should be to reconstruct a picture of the character of the child when it was born in order to study which of the traits he finds in the analysand are part of the original nature and which are acquired through influential circumstances; furthermore, which of the acquired qualities conflict with the genetic ones and which tend to reinforce them. What we find very often is that by the wish of the parents (personally and as representatives of society) the child is forced to repress or to weaken his original dispositions and to replace them by those traits which society wants it to develop. At this point we find the roots of neurotic developments; the person develops a sense of false identity. While genuine identity rests upon the awareness of one's suchness in terms of the person one is born as, pseudo-identity rests upon the personality which society has imposed upon us. Hence a person is in constant need of approval in order to keep his balance. Genuine identity does not need such approval because the person's picture of himself is identical with his authentic personality structure.

The discovery of the significance of early childhood events in the development of a person leads easily to an underestimation of the importance of later events. According to Freudian theory the character of a person was more or less completely formed at the age of seven or eight and hence fundamental changes in later years were supposed to be virtually impossible. Empirical data, however, seem to show that this assumption exaggerates the role of childhood. To be sure, if the conditions which have helped to form the character of a person in childhood continue, the character structure is likely to remain the same. It must further be admitted that this in fact holds true for most people who in later life continue to live under conditions similar to those that existed in their childhood. But Freud's assumption has deflected the attention from those cases in which radical changes have occurred in people through radically new experiences they have had. Take, for instance, those who throughout their childhood were convinced that nobody would ever care for them unless he or she wanted something from them, that there was no sympathy or love which was not the payment for services or a bribe to perform them. A person may go through life without ever having experienced that somebody cares or is interested and does not want anything in return. But when it happens that such a person experiences another person's having a real interest without wanting anything, this might drastically change such character traits as suspicion, fear, the feeling of being unlovable, et cetera. (Of course, from the bourgeois viewpoint of Freud, and his lack of belief in love, this kind of experience was not to be expected.) In very drastic cases of character change one can speak even of genuine conversions, which means a complete change in values, expectations and attitudes because something entirely new has occurred in the life of the converted person. And yet such conversions are not possible unless the person already has the potentiality within himself that becomes manifest in his conversion. I admit that the superficial evidence does not speak for such an assumption because people usually do not change, but one has to consider that most people do not experience anything that is truly new. They usually find what they expect to find, and hence are barred from the possibility of a fundamentally new experience bringing about fundamental character changes.

The difficulty of discovering what a person was like at the moment of birth and in the first months or the first year lies in the fact that hardly anybody remembers what he or she felt or was at the time. The first memories usually do not go back earlier than the first two or three years and herein lies one of the crucial difficulties of Freud's assumption of the significance of early childhood. He tried to cope with this difficulty by study of the transference. This is sometimes successful but if one studies the case histories of the Freudian school one is forced to acknowledge that much of what are supposed to be experiences of the earliest childhood are reconstructions. And these reconstructions are very unreliable. They are based on the postulates of Freud's theory, and the conviction of authenticity is often the product of a subtle kind of brainwashing. While the analyst is supposed to remain on the empirical level, in reality in a subtle way he suggests to the patient what the latter is supposed to have experienced and after a long analysis and on the basis of dependency on the analyst, the patient will very often proclaim—or as one reads sometimes in analytic case histories "admit"—that he can genuinely feel the correctness of what the theoretical construction expects him to feel. To be sure the analyst should let the patient be free from all persuasion. But the sensitive patient, or even the not-so-sensitive one, catches on after a while to what the analyst expects to hear and consents to an interpretation that only gives in to the analyst's construction of what is supposed to have happened. Furthermore, it must be considered that the expectations of the analyst are based not only on the demands of the theory but also on the demands of the bourgeois picture of what the "normal" person is like. Assuming, for instance, that in a person the wish for freedom and the protest against being determined by heteronomous demands are particularly strongly developed, it would be considered that the very rebelliousness of this person has an irrational quality and is to be explained by the Oedipal hatred of the son toward the father, the root of which is the sexual rivalry for the mother-wife. The fact that children are controlled and manipulated in childhood and later on in life is assumed to be normal and rebelliousness therefore the expression of irrationality.

I wish to add another complicating factor, to which little attention has been paid. The relationship between parents and children is usually seen as a one-way street, namely the effect parents have upon children. But what is often ignored is that this influence is by no means one-sided. A parent may have a natural dislike for a child and even for a newborn baby, not only for reasons which are often discussed—that it is an unwanted child or that the parent is destructive, sadistic, et cetera—but for the reason that child and parent just are not compatible by their very natures, and that in this respect the relationship is no different from that between grown-up people. The parent may just have a dislike for the kind of child he or she produced and the child may feel this dislike from the very beginning. On the other hand, the child may have a dislike for the kind of parents he has and being the weaker he is punished for his dislike by all kinds of more or less subtle sanctions. The child—and equally the mother —is forced into a situation where the mother has to take care of the child and the child has to accept the mother in spite of the fact that they heartily dislike each other. The child cannot articulate this; the mother would feel guilty if she admitted to herself that she did not like a child she gave birth to, and so both behave under a special kind of pressure and punish each other for being forced into an unwanted intimacy. The mother pretends to love the child and subtly punishes it for being forced to do so, the child pretends in some way or another to love the mother because his life depends so totally on her. In such a situation a great deal of dishonesty develops which the children often express in their own indirect ways of rebellion and which the mothers usually negate because they feel that nothing could be more shameful than not to like one's own children.

3. Freud's Theory of Dream Interpretation

If Freud had not created a theory of neurosis and a method of therapy he would still be one of the most outstanding figures in the science of man because he discovered the art of dream interpretation. To be sure, in almost any epoch people have tried to interpret dreams. How could it be otherwise when people wake up in the morning and remember the peculiar experiences they had during sleep? There were many methods of interpreting dreams, some of them based on superstitions and irrational ideas, others with a deep understanding of the significance of the dream. This understanding has not been more clearly expressed than in the Talmudic statement "A dream which has not been interpreted is like a letter that has not been opened." This sentence expresses the recognition that a dream is a message which we send to ourselves and which we have to understand in order to understand ourselves. Yet in spite of the long history of dream interpretation, Freud was the first one to give the interpretation such a systematic and scientific basis. He gave us the tools for the understanding of dreams, which anybody can use provided he learns how to handle them.

One can hardly exaggerate the significance of dream interpretation. First of all it makes us aware of feelings and thoughts that exist within ourselves and yet which we are not aware of while we are awake. The dream, as Freud once put it, is the royal way to the understanding of the unconscious. Secondly the dream is a creative act in which the average person demonstrates creative powers of whose existence he has no idea when he is awake. Freud discovered, furthermore, that our dreams are not the simple expression of unconscious strivings but that they are usually distorted by the influence of a subtle censorship which is even present when we are asleep and forces us to distort the true meaning of our dream thoughts (the "latent dream"). Thus the censor is deceived, as it were, and permits the hidden thoughts to pass the frontier to consciousness if they are sufficiently disguised. This concept led Freud to the assumption that every dream (with the exception of children's dreams) is distorted and has to be restored to its original meaning by dream interpretation.

Freud developed a general theory of dreams. He assumed that man during the night has many impulses and desires, especially of a sexual nature, which would interrupt his sleep were it not that he experiences these wishes as fulfilled in the dream and hence does not have to wake up to seek realistic satisfaction. Dreams were for Freud the disguised expression of fulfillment of sexual wishes. Dream as wish-fulfillment was the fundamental insight which Freud brought to the field of dream interpretation.

One obvious objection to this theory is that we have many nightmares which would be difficult to explain as fulfillment of a desire, since they are painful to the point of sometimes interrupting sleep. But Freud took care of this argument in an ingenious way. He pointed out that there are sadistic or masochistic wishes which produce great anxiety but are still wishes which the dream satisfies even though another part of us is frightened of them.

The consistency of Freud's system of dream interpretation is so striking that his concepts are very impressive as a working hypothesis. If, however, one does not share Freud's basic assumption about sex, a few other considerations recommend themselves. Instead of assuming that the dream is the distorted presentation of a wish, one may formulate the hypothesis that the dream represents any feeling, wish, fear or thought that is sufficiently important to be present during our sleep, and that its appearance in dreams is a sign of its importance. In my observation of dreams, I have found that many dreams do not contain a wish but offer an insight into one's own situation or into the personality of others. In order to appreciate this function one must consider the particularity of the state of sleep. During sleep we are liberated from the task of sustaining our existence by work or by defending ourselves against possible dangers. (Only signals of an emergency wake us up from our sleep.) We are not under the influence of the social "noise," by which I mean the opinion of others, common nonsense and common pathology. Perhaps one could say that sleep is the only situation where we are really free. This has consequences: we see the world subjectively and not from the viewpoint that guides us in our waking life objectively—that is to say, as we must see it in order to manipulate it. For instance, in a dream the element of fire might express love or destructiveness, but that is a different fire from the one on which one can bake a cake. The dream is poetic and it speaks the universal language of symbolism which is basically common to all times and all cultures. It is, together with poetry and art, a universal language which mankind has developed. In the dream we do not see the world as we have to see it when we want to manipulate it; rather, we see the poetic meaning it has for us.

This insight into the nature of the dream, however, was greatly restricted by the peculiarity of Freud's personality. Freud was a rationalist with a lack of artistic or poetic inclination, and hence he had almost no feeling for symbolic language whether expressed in dreams or in poetry. The lack forced upon him a very narrow concept of symbols. He either understood them as sexual —and the range of possibilities in this respect is great, since a line and a circle are exceedingly widespread forms of symbolism—or he understood them only by finding out through associations with what else they were connected. It is one of the most peculiar contradictions that Freud, the expert of the irrational and symbolic, himself was so little capable of understanding symbols. This becomes particularly blatant if we compare Freud with one of the greatest interpreters of symbols, Johann Jakob Bachofen, the discoverer of the matriarchal society. For Bachofen a symbol had a richness and depth which went far beyond the word *symbol.* He could have written many many pages on one symbol—for instance, the egg—while Freud would have interpreted this symbol as "obviously" expressing an aspect of sexual life. For Freud a dream required an almost endless sequence of associations to its various parts, and very often we do not know much more about the meaning of the dream after having gone through this process of interpretation than we knew before.

THE ROLE OF ASSOCIATIONS IN DREAM INTERPRETATION

In order to give an example of Freud's method of association I quote a dream *in extenso,* and its interpretation. It is a dream which Freud himself dreamt and hence part of his self-analysis (Freud, 1900a, pp. 170–4):

DREAM OF THE BOTANICAL MONOGRAPH

I had written a monograph on a certain plant. The book lay before me and I was at the moment turning over a folded coloured plate. Bound up in each copy there was a dried specimen of the plant, as though it had been taken from a herbarium.

ANALYSIS

That morning I had seen a new book in the window of a book-shop, bearing the title *The Genus Cyclamen*—evidently a *monograph* on that plant.

Cyclamens, I reflected, were my wife's *favourite flowers* and I reproached myself for so rarely remembering to *bring* her *flowers,* which was what she liked.—The subject of *"bringing flowers"* re-called an anecdote which I had recently repeated to a circle of friends and which I had used as evidence in favour of my theory that forgetting is very often determined by an unconscious pur-pose and that it always enables one to deduce the secret intentions of the person who forgets.* A young woman was accustomed to receiving a bouquet of flowers from her husband on her birthday. One year this token of his affection failed to appear, and she burst into tears. Her husband came in and had no idea why she was crying till she told him that to-day was her birthday. He clasped his hand to his head and exclaimed: "I'm so sorry, but I'd quite forgotten. I'll go out at once and fetch your *flowers.* " But she was not to be consoled; for she recognized that her husband's forget-fulness was a proof that she no longer had the same place in his thoughts as she had formerly.—This lady, Frau L., had met my wife two days before I had the dream, had told her that she was feeling quite well and enquired after me. Some years ago she had come to me for treatment.

I now made a fresh start. Once, I recalled, I really *had* written something in the nature of a *monograph on a plant,* namely a dis-sertation on the *coca-plant* [1884], which had drawn Karl Koller's attention to the anaesthetic properties of cocaine. I had myself indicated this application of the alkaloid in my published paper, but I had not been thorough enough to pursue the matter fur-ther. This reminded me that on the morning of the day after the dream—I had not found time to interpret it till the evening—I had thought about cocaine in a kind of daydream. If ever I got glaucoma, I had thought, I should travel to Berlin and get myself operated on, incognito, in my friend's [Fliess's] house, by a sur-

---

*The theory was published a few months after the date of the dream (in Freud, 1898b) and then incorporated in *The Psychopathology of Everyday Life* (Freud, 1901b).—E.F.

geon recommended by him. The operating surgeon, who would have no idea of my identity, would boast once again of how easily such operations could be performed since the introduction of cocaine; and I should not give the slightest hint that I myself had had a share in the discovery. This phantasy had led on to reflections of how awkward it is, when all is said and done, for a physician to ask for medical treatment for himself from his professional colleagues. The Berlin eye-surgeon would not know me, and I should be able to pay his fees like anyone else. It was not until I had recalled this day-dream that I realized that the recollection of a specific event lay behind it. Shortly after Koller's discovery, my father had in fact been attacked by glaucoma; my friend Dr. Königstein, the ophthalmic surgeon, had operated on him; while Dr. Koller had been in charge of the cocaine anaesthesia and had commented on the fact that this case had brought together all of the three men who had had a share in the introduction of cocaine.

My thoughts then went on to the occasion when I had last been reminded of this business of the cocaine. It had been a few days earlier, when I had been looking at a copy of a *Festschrift* in which grateful pupils had celebrated the jubilee of their teacher and laboratory director. Among the laboratory's claims to distinction which were enumerated in this book I had seen a mention of the fact that Koller had made his discovery there of the anaesthetic properties of cocaine. I then suddenly perceived that my dream was connected with an event of the previous evening. I had walked home precisely with Dr. Königstein and had got into conversation with him about a matter which never fails to excite my feelings whenever it is raised. While I was talking to him in the entrance-hall, Professor *Gärtner* (Gardener) and his wife had joined us; and I could not help congratulating them both on their *blooming* looks. But Professor Gärtner was one of the authors of the *Festschrift* I have just mentioned, and may well have reminded me of it. Moreover, the Frau L., whose disappointment on her birthday I described earlier, was mentioned—though only, it is true, in another connection—in my conversation with Dr. Königstein.

I will make an attempt at interpreting the other determinants of the content of the dream as well. There was a *dried specimen of the plant* included in the monograph, as though it had been a *her-*

barium. This led me to a memory from my secondary school. Our headmaster once called together the boys from the higher forms and handed over the school's herbarium to them to be looked through and cleaned. Some small *worms*—book-worms—had found their way into it. He does not seem to have had much confidence in my helpfulness for he handed me only a few sheets. These, as I could still recall, included some Crucifers. I never had a specially intimate contact with botany. In my preliminary examination in botany I was also given a Crucifer to identify—and failed to do so. My prospects would not have been too bright, if I had not been helped out by my theoretical knowledge. I went on from the Cruciferae to the Compositae. It occurred to me that artichokes were Compositae, and indeed I might fairly have called them my *favourite flowers.* Being more generous than I am, my wife often brought me back those favourite flowers of mine from the market.

I saw the monograph which I had written *lying before me.* This again led me back to something. I had had a letter from my friend [Fliess] in Berlin the day before in which he had shown his power of visualization: "I am very much occupied with your dream-book. *I see it lying finished before me and I see myself turning over its pages.* "[1] How much I envied him his gift as a seer! If only *I* could have seen it lying finished before me!

The folded coloured plate. While I was a medical student I was the constant victim of an impulse only to learn things out of *monographs.* In spite of my limited means, I succeeded in getting hold of a number of volumes of the proceedings of medical societies and was enthralled by their *coloured plates.* I was proud of my hankering for thoroughness. When I myself had begun to publish papers, I had been obliged to make my own drawings to illustrate them and I remembered that one of them had been so wretched that a friendly colleague had jeered at me over it. There followed, I could not quite make out how, a recollection from very early youth. It had once amused my father to hand over a book with *coloured plates* (an account of a journey through Persia) for me and my eldest sister to destroy. Not easy to justify from the educational

---

[1]Freud's reply to this letter from Fliess is dated March 10, 1898 (Freud, 1950a, Letter 84); so that the dream must have occurred not more than a day or two earlier.

point of view! I had been five years old at the time and my sister not yet three; and the picture of the two of us blissfully pulling the book to pieces (leaf by leaf, like an *artichoke,* I found myself saying) was almost the only plastic memory that I retained from that period of my life. Then, when I became a student, I had developed a passion for collecting and owning books, which was analogous to my liking for learning out of monographs: *a favourite hobby.* (The idea of *"favourite"* had already appeared in connection with cyclamens and artichokes.) I had become a *book-worm.* I had always, from the time I first began to think about myself, referred this first passion of mine back to the childhood memory I have mentioned. Or rather, I had recognized that the childhood scene was a "screen memory" for my later bibliophile propensities (Cf. my paper on screen memories in Freud, 1898a). And I had early discovered, of course, that passions often lead to sorrow. When I was seventeen I had run up a largish account at the bookseller's and had nothing to meet it with; and my father had scarcely taken it as an excuse that my inclinations might have chosen a worse outlet. The recollection of this experience from the later years of my youth at once brought back to my mind the conversation with my friend Dr. Königstein. For in the course of it we had discussed the same question of my being blamed for being too much absorbed in my *favourite hobbies.*

For reasons with which we are not concerned, I shall not pursue the interpretation of this dream any further, but will merely indicate the direction in which it lay. In the course of the work of analysis I was reminded of my conversation with Dr. Königstein, and I was brought to it from more than one direction. When I take into account the topics touched upon in that conversation, the meaning of the dream becomes intelligible to me. All the trains of thought starting from the dream—the thoughts about my wife's and my own favourite flowers, about cocaine, about the awkwardness of medical treatment among colleagues, about my preference for studying monographs and about my neglect of certain branches of science such as botany—all of these trains of thought, when they were further pursued, led ultimately to one or other of the many ramifications of my conversation with Dr. Königstein. Once again the dream, like the one we first analyzed—the dream of Irma's injection—turns out to have been in the nature of a self-justification, a plea on behalf of my own rights. Indeed, it carried the subject that was raised in the earlier dream a stage further and discussed it with reference to fresh material that had arisen in the interval between the two dreams. Even the apparently indifferent form in which the dream was couched turns out to have had significance. What is meant was: "After all, I'm the man who wrote the valuable and memorable paper (on cocaine)" just as in the earlier dream I had said on my behalf: "I'm a conscientious and hard-working student." In both cases what I was insisting was: "I may allow myself to do this." There is, however, no need for me to carry the interpretation of the dream any further, since my only purpose in reporting it was to illustrate by an example the relation between the content of a dream and the experience of the previous day which provoked it. So long as I was aware only of the dream's *manifest* content, it appeared to be related only to a *single* event of the dream-day. But when the analysis was carried out, a *second* source of the dream emerged in another experience of the same day. The first of these two impressions with which the dream was connected was an indifferent one, a subsidiary circumstance: I had seen a book in a shop-window whose title attracted my attention for a moment but whose subject-matter could scarcely be of inter- est to me. The second experience had a high degree of psychical importance: I had a good hour's lively conversation with my friend the eye-surgeon; in the course of it I had given him some informa- tion which was bound to affect both of us closely, and I had had memories stirred up in me which had drawn my attention to a great variety of internal stresses in my own mind. Moreover, the conversation had been interrupted before its conclusion because we had been joined by acquaintances.

If we analyze Freud's analysis of the dream what do we find? He brings various associations to the dream, one about the young woman who complained of her husband's having forgotten to bring her flowers on her birthday, another about his dissertation on the coca plant which had drawn Karl Koller's attention to the anaesthetic qualities of cocaine. The dried plant leads to associa- tions from his school life where the teacher had given him the task of cleaning a herbarium. Seeing the monograph lying before him reminds him of something his friend Fliess had written him the day before and the folded colored plates lead to an association about his aptitude for making them and his propensity for buying books. He goes on to talk about a conversation with Dr. Königstein.

If we ask what insight we have into Freud from his interpretation of the dream I am afraid we must admit that we learn almost nothing about him. And yet the meaning of the dream is so obvious and indeed exceedingly important as a key to understanding Freud's personality.

A flower is a symbol of love, Eros, friendship and joy. What has Freud done with love and joy? He has transformed them into objects of scientific research; love and joy have been removed from the flower which is now dried and an object of scientific research. What could be more characteristic of Freud's whole life? He has transformed love (in his own terms, sexuality) into an object of scientific observation and in this process it has dried up and lost its meaning as human experience. This is what Freud expresses so clearly in this dream and yet by heaping association upon association which end up in practically nothing, he succeeds in covering up the awareness of the meaning of the dream: the transformation of love from life to an object of science. This dream, like many others, is an example of the fact that Freud, by innumerable associations, succeeds very often in covering up the real meaning of the dream because he does not want to see this meaning. To put it differently, Freud's method of endless associations is an expression of resistance against the understanding of the meaning of his dreams.

THE LIMITATIONS OF FREUD'S INTERPRETATION OF HIS OWN DREAMS

The following dream does not show the features of the method mentioned above, the heaping up of endless associations. The use of associations here is relatively simple and what is remarkable is the resistance Freud exhibits against the interpretation of rather obvious material in the dream. "In the spring of 1897," Freud writes (1900a, pp. 136–42),

> I learnt that two professors at our university had recommended me for appointment as *professor extraordinarius*. [1] The news surprised and greatly delighted me, since it implied recognition by two eminent men, which could not be put down to any considerations of a personal kind. But I at once warned myself not to attach any expectations to the event. During the last few years the Ministry had disregarded recommendations of that sort; and several of my colleagues who were my seniors in age and at least my equals in merit had been waiting vainly for an appointment. I had no reason to believe that I should be more fortunate. I therefore determined to meet the future with resignation. So far as I knew, I was not an ambitious man; I was following my profession with gratifying success even without the advantages afforded by a title. Moreover there was no question of my pronouncing the grapes sweet or sour; they hung far too high over my head.
>
> One evening I had a visit from a friend—one of the men whose example I had taken as a warning to me. For a considerable time he had been a candidate for promotion to a professorship, a rank which in our society turns its holder into a demi-god to his patients. Less resigned than I was, however, he was in the habit of paying his respects from time to time in the offices of the Ministry with a view to advancing his prospects. He had been paying one of these visits just before calling on me. He told me that on this occasion he had driven the exalted official into a corner and had asked straight out whether the delay over his appointment was not in fact due to denominational considerations. The reply had been that, in view of the present state of feeling, it was no doubt true that, for the moment, His Excellency was not in a position, etc. etc. "At least I know where I am now," my friend had concluded. It was not news to me, though it was bound to strengthen my feeling of

[1]Roughly equivalent to an assistant professor. All such appointments in Austria were made by the minister of education. The fact of this recommendation is reported by Freud in a letter to Fliess of February 8, 1897 (Freud, 1950a, letter 58) and the dream itself is mentioned on March 15, 1894 (ibid., letter 85). The "denominational considerations" mentioned below relate of course, to anti-Semitic feeling, which was ripe in Vienna during the last years of the nineteenth century.

resignation; for the same denominational considerations applied to my own case.

On the morning after this visit I had the following dream, which was remarkable among other things for its form. It consisted of two thoughts and two pictures—each thought being succeeded by a picture. I shall, however, report only the first half of the dream here, since the other half has no connection with the purpose for which I am describing the dream.

I. . . . My friend R. was my uncle.—I had a great feeling of affection for him.

II. I saw before me his face, somewhat changed. It was as though it had been drawn out lengthways. A yellow beard that surrounded it stood out especially clearly.

Then followed the two other pieces which I shall pass over—once more a thought followed by a picture.

The interpretation of the dream took place as follows.

When, during the course of the morning, the dream came into my head, I laughed aloud and said: "The dream's nonsense!" But it refused to go away and followed me about all day, till at last in the evening I began to reproach myself: "If one of your patients who was interpreting a dream could find nothing better to say than that it was nonsense, you would take him up about it and suspect that the dream had some disagreeable story at the back of it which he wanted to avoid becoming aware of. Treat yourself in the same way. Your opinion that the dream is nonsense only means that you have an internal resistance against interpreting it. Don't let yourself be put off like this." So I set about the interpretation.

"*R. was my uncle.*" What could that mean? I never had more than one uncle—Uncle Josef.* There was an unhappy story attached to him. Once—more than thirty years ago,—in his eagerness to make money, he allowed himself to be involved in a transaction of a kind that is severely punished by the law, and he was in fact punished for it. My father, whose hair turned grey from grief in a few days, used always to say that Uncle Josef was not a bad man but only a simpleton; those were his words. So that if my friend R. was my Uncle Josef, what I was meaning to say was that R. was a simpleton.

---

*It is astonishing to observe the way in which my memory—my waking memory—was narrowed at this point, for the purposes of the analysis. Actually I have known five of my uncles, and loved and honoured one of them. But at the moment at which I overcame my resistance to interpreting the dream I said to myself that I never had more than one uncle—the one that was intended in the dream.

Hardly credible and most disagreeable!—But there was the face which I saw in the dream with its elongated features and yellow beard. My uncle did in fact have a face like that, elongated and framed in a handsome fair beard. My friend R. had originally been extremely dark; but when black-haired people begin to turn grey they pay for the splendour of their youth. Hair by hair, their black beards go through an unpleasing change of colour: first they turn to a reddish brown, and only then to a definite grey. My friend R.'s beard was at that time passing through this stage—and so, incidentally, was my own, as I had noticed with dissatisfaction. The face that I saw in the dream was at once my friend R.'s and my uncle's. It was like one of Galton's composite photographs. (In order to bring out family likenesses, Galton used to photograph several faces on the same plate. . . .) So there could be no doubt that I really did mean that my friend R. was a simpleton—like my Uncle Josef.

I still had no idea at all what could be the purpose of this comparison, against which I continued to struggle. It did not go very deep, after all, since my uncle was a criminal, whereas my friend R. bore an unblemished character . . . except for having been fined for knocking a boy down with his bicycle. Could I have had that crime in mind? That would have been making fun of the comparison. At this point I remembered another conversation which I had had a few days earlier with another colleague, N., and, now I came to think of it, upon the same subject. I had met N. in the street. He too had been recommended for a professorship. He had heard of the honour that had been paid me and had offered me his congratulations on it; but I had unhesitatingly refused to accept them. "You are the last person," I had said, "to make that kind of joke; you know what such a recommendation is worth from your own experience." "Who can say?" he had answered—jokingly, it seemed; "there was something definite against *me*. Don't you know that a woman once started legal proceedings against me? I needn't assure you that the case was dismissed. It was a disgraceful attempt at blackmail; and I had the greatest difficulty in saving the prosecutrix from being punished. But perhaps they may be using this at the Ministry as an excuse for not appointing me. But *you* have an unblemished character." This told me who the criminal was, and at the same time showed me how the dream was to be interpreted and what its purpose was. My Uncle Josef represented my two colleagues who had not been appointed to professorships—the one as a simpleton and the other as a criminal. I now saw too why they were represented in this light. If the appointment of my friends R. and N. had been postponed for "denominational" reasons, my own appointment was also open to doubt; if, however, I could attribute the rejection of my two friends to other reasons, which did not apply to me, my hopes would remain untouched. This was the procedure adopted by my dream: it made one of them, R., into a simpleton and the other, N., into a criminal, whereas *I* was neither the one nor the other; thus we no longer had anything in common; I could rejoice at my appointment to a professorship, and I could avoid drawing the distressing conclusion that R.'s report of what the high official had said to him must apply equally to me.

But I felt obliged to proceed still further with my interpretation of the dream; I felt I had not yet finished dealing with it satisfactorily. I was still uneasy over the light-heartedness with which I had degraded two of my respected colleagues in order to keep open my own path to a professorship. My dissatisfaction with my conduct, however, had diminished since I had come to realize the worth that was to be attached to expressions in dreams. I was prepared to deny through thick and thin that I really considered that R. was a simpleton and that I really disbelieved N.'s account of the blackmailing affair. Nor did I believe that Irma was really made dangerously ill through being injected with Otto's preparation of propyl. In both these cases what my dreams had expressed was only *my wish that it might be so.* The assertion in which my wish was realized sounded less absurd in the later dream than in the earlier one; it made cleverer use of the actual facts in its construction, like a well-designed slander of the kind that makes people feel that "there's something in it." For one of the professors in his own faculty had voted against my friend R., and my friend N. had himself innocently provided me with the material for my aspersions. Nevertheless, I must repeat, the dream seemed to me to stand in need of further elucidation.

I then recalled that there was still a piece of the dream which the interpretation had not touched. After the idea had occurred to me that R. was my uncle, I had had a warm feeling of affection for him in the dream. Where did that feeling belong? I had naturally never had any feeling of affection for my Uncle Josef. I had been fond of my friend R. and had esteemed him for many years; but if I had gone up to him and expressed my sentiments in terms approaching the degree of affection I had felt in the dream, there could be no doubt that he would have been astonished. My affection for him struck me as ungenuine and exaggerated—like the judgement of his intellectual qualities which I had expressed by fusing his personality with my uncle's, though *there* the exaggeration had been in the opposite direction. But a new light began to dawn on me. The affection in the dream did not belong to the latent content, to the thoughts that lay behind the dream; it stood in contradiction to them and was calculated to conceal the true interpretation of the dream. And probably that was precisely its *raison d'être.* I recalled my resistance against embarking on the interpretation, how long I had put it off and how I had declared that the dream was sheer nonsense. My psycho-analytic treatments taught me how a repudiation of that kind was to be interpreted: it had no value as a judgement but was simply an expression of emotion. If my little daughter did not want an apple that was offered to her, she asserted that the apple tasted sour without having tasted it. And if my patients behaved like the child, I knew that they were concerned with an idea which they wanted to repress. The same was true of my dream. I did not want to interpret it, because the interpretation contained something that I was struggling against —namely, the assertion that R. was a simpleton. The affection that I felt for R. could not be derived from the latent dream-thoughts; but no doubt it originated from this struggle of mine. If my dream was distorted in this respect from its latent content—and distorted into its opposite,—then the affection that was manifest in the dream served the purpose of this distortion. In other words, distortion was shown in this case to be deliberate and to be a means of *dissimulation.* My dream thoughts had contained a slander against R.; and, in order that I might not notice this, what appeared in the dream was the opposite, a feeling of affection for him.

It seemed as though this might be a discovery of general validity. It is true that, as was shown by the instances quoted in Chapter III ["A Dream is the Fulfillment of a Wish"], there are some dreams which are undisguised fulfillments of wishes. But in cases where the wish-fulfillment is unrecognizable, where it has been disguised, there must have existed some inclination to put up a defence against the wish; and owing to this defence the wish was unable to express itself except in a distorted shape. I will try to seek a social parallel to this internal event in the mind. Where can we find a similar distortion of a psychical act in social life? Only where two persons are concerned, one of whom possesses a certain degree of power which the second is obliged to take into account. In such a case the second person will distort his psychical acts or, as we might put it, will dissimulate. The politeness which I practise every day is to a large extent dissimulation of this kind; and when I interpret my dreams for my readers I am obliged to adopt similar distortions.

Freud correctly interpets the dream that his friend R. was his uncle as expressing a derogatory feeling about R., since his uncle had been somewhat of a criminal. Freud interprets the dream on the basis of some simple associations with two colleagues of his who might have been appointed to professorships but were not given this honor because one was a simpleton and the other a criminal. Thus their appointment was not bypassed because they were Jews, and Freud is given more hope that he might be made a professor. Freud speaks of the strong resistance he felt to interpreting this dream, and incidentally mentions the fact that he distorts the interpretation of his own dreams for his readers for reasons of "politeness." What Freud apparently omits here is the fact that his dream means that the strength of his wish to become a professor makes him wish that two Jewish competitors do not become professors, for reasons other than their religious faith. Freud later returns to this dream, illustrating his assumption that the child's wishes and impulses live on in it. Not having recognized that the degradation of his friends has been caused by his own wish to be appointed professor, he writes that "the affection I felt in the dream for my friend R. was a product of opposition and revolt against slanders upon my two colleagues which were contained in the dream thoughts." But he goes on to say (Freud, 1900a, p. 191f.):

> The dream was one of my own; I may therefore continue its analysis by saying that my feelings were not yet satisfied by the solution that had so far been reached. I knew that my waking judgement upon the colleagues who were so ill-used in the dream thoughts would have been a very different one; and the force of my wish not

to share their fate in the matter of the appointment struck me as insufficient to explain the contradiction between my waking and dreaming estimates of them. If it was indeed true that my craving to be addressed with a different title was as strong as all that, it showed a pathological ambition which I did not recognize in myself and which I believed was alien to me. I could not tell how other people who believed they knew me would judge me in this respect. It might be that I was really ambitious; but, if so, my ambition had long ago been transferred to objects quite other than the title and rank of *professor extraordinarius.*

This last statement sounds rather strong. It follows the logic "There cannot be what must not be." Freud believes he is not particularly ambitious. The formulation of the decisive sentence is interesting. He speaks of the "craving to be addressed with a different title" and thereby camouflages the whole problem. As he said earlier, the professor was a demigod to his patients. The appointment was of the greatest importance for his social prestige and at least for his income. With the innocent formulation "to be addressed with a different title," as if that meant very little, Freud still denies his ambition to be appointed professor. Furthermore he insists that pathological ambition is alien to him; by calling it pathological he again covers up the situation. What is pathological about the ambition to be a professor, an aim which, as he says elsewhere, is quite important to him? On the contrary such ambition is quite normal. He leaves it open to other people to judge him in this respect but he limits them to "people who believed they knew me" rather than "who knew me" and eventually he minimizes the whole problem by saying that if he was ambitious the "ambition had long ago been transferred to objects quite other than the title and rank of *professor extraordinarius.*"

Then, however, Freud rephrases his own words, speaking of the ambitiousness that produced the dream and raising the question what its origin might be. Answering this question he speaks of an event in his childhood when a professional soothsayer had predicted that one day he would become a cabinet minister. (This was the time of the "Bürger" ministry in which even some ministers were Jews.) In other words a bright Jewish boy had a chance to become a cabinet minister. Freud continues: "The events of that period no doubt had some bearing on the fact that up to a time shortly before I entered the University it had been my intention to study Law; it was only at the last moment that I changed my mind" (ibid, p. 192). Indeed this is pretty strong proof of Freud's ambition for fame, and the world would have lost the gifts of this genius had he decided to become a lawyer. Freud goes further in saying that the dream is really the fulfillment of his own wish to become a minister. "In mishandling my two learned and eminent colleagues because they were Jews, and in treating the one as a simpleton and the other as a criminal, I was behaving as though I were the Minister, I had put myself in the Minister's place. Turning the tables on His Excellency with a vengeance! He had refused to appoint me *professor extraordinarius* and I had retaliated in the dream by stepping into his shoes" (ibid., p. 192f.).* Freud, who so firmly denies his ambition as an adult, asserts that the ambitions are really those of the child and not of the adult.

We find here one of the premises of Freud's thinking. Those features that are considered incompatible with a respectable professional man like Freud are relegated to childhood, and it is implied that inasmuch as they belong to childhood experiences they do not represent the experience of the adult. The assumption that all neurotic tendencies arise in childhood is in fact the protection of the adult from the suspicion of being neurotic. Freud was indeed a very neurotic man but it was impossible for him to conceive of himself as such and at the same time to feel his was a normal respectable profession. Hence everything that

*In an amusing letter to Fliess of March 11, 1902 (Freud, 1950a, letter 152), Freud tells the story of how he came actually to be appointed to a professorship, two years after the publication of this book.

did not fit into the pattern of the normal man was considered to be childhood material and this childhood material was not considered to be still fully alive and present in the adult. (This of course has all changed in the last fifty years, since neurosis has become respectable, and the model of the rational, healthy, normal adult bourgeois has been dismissed from the cultural scene. But for Freud it was still very strong and only if one understands it fully can one understand Freud's tendency to exclude everything irrational from his adult life. This is one of the reasons why his so-called self-analysis was a failure, since he usually did not see what he did not want to see—namely, what did not fit into the picture of the rational, respectable bourgeois.)

A central element in Freud's dream interpretation is the concept of censorship. Freud discovered that many dreams tend to hide their true meaning and express it in forms which are not dissimilar to a political writer in a dictatorship, who expresses his thought between the lines or speaks about an event in classical Greece while really referring to contemporary events. Thus for Freud, the dream is never an open communication but is to be compared to a coded writing which has to be deciphered in order to be understandable. The coding has to be done in such a way that even the dreamer feels safe when he expresses ideas in his dream which do not fit into the thought patterns of the society in which he lives. By saying this I wish to emphasize that the censorship has more of a social character than Freud assumed, but at the moment this is of no importance. What matters is Freud's insight that the dream must be decoded. However, this insight in its simple and dogmatic formulation often led to erroneous results. Not every dream needs to be decoded and the degree of coding differs very much from dream to dream.

Whether and to what extent coding is necessary depends on the sanctions which society puts against those who think unthinkable thoughts in their sleep and it also depends on such individual factors as how submissive and frightened a person is, and hence to what degree he feels in need of coding a thought which can be dangerous. When I say dangerous I do not refer particularly to external sanctions of society against those who have dangerous thoughts. Indeed that happens too, and is not invalidated by the objection that after all our sleep thoughts—that is, our dreams—are secret and nobody knows about them. If it is important to avoid dangerous thoughts one must not even think them in one's dreams because they must remain deeply repressed. By dangerous thoughts, I mean thoughts which a person would be punished or might suffer in his daily life for having, if they were known. There are such thoughts, as we all know, and people have a good sense of what they had better not say and hence had better not think if they do not want to suffer disadvantages. However, I am speaking here mainly of thoughts which are dangerous not because they say something specific which would be sanctioned, but because they move out of the frame of reference of common sense. They are thoughts which are not shared by anybody else or by more than a very small group and hence they put a person in the position of feeling isolated, alone, out of contact. It is this very experience which contains the nucleus of insanity which occurs when a person has cut off completely any connection with others.

Significant as Freud's discovery of the operation of the censor was, it also damaged our understanding of dreams when it was applied dogmatically and in reference to every single dream.

Symbolic Language of Dreams

Before continuing the discussion of whether every dream is as distorted as Freud assumes, it is useful to distinguish between two kinds of symbols, *universal* and *accidental.* The accidental symbol has no intrinsic relationship to that which it symbolizes. Let us assume that someone has had a saddening experience in a certain city; when he hears the name of that city, he will easily connect the name with a mood of sadness, just as he would connect it with a mood of joy had his experience been a happy one. Quite obviously there is nothing in the nature of the city that is either sad or joyful. It is the individual experience connected with the city that makes it a symbol of a mood. The same reaction could occur in connection with a house, a street, a dress, certain scenery or anything once connected with a specific mood. The picture in the dream represents this mood, the city "stands for" the mood once experienced in it. Here the connection between the symbol and the experience symbolized is entirely accidental.

As a result, we need associations of the dreamer in order to understand what the accidental symbol means. Had he not told us about the experience he had in the city of which he dreamed or about the connection between the person he dreams of and his experiences with this person, we could not possibly understand what these symbols mean.

The *universal* symbol, on the contrary, is one in which there is an intrinsic relationship between the symbol and that which it represents. Take, for instance, the symbol of fire. We are fascinated by certain qualities of fire in a fireplace. First of all, by its aliveness. It changes continuously, it moves all the time, and yet there is constancy in it. It remains the same without being the same. It gives the impression of power, of grace and lightness. It is as if it were dancing and had an inexhaustible source of energy. When we use fire as a symbol, we describe the inner experience characterized by the same elements which we notice in the sensory experience of fire: the mood of energy, lightness, movement, grace, gaiety—sometimes one, sometimes another of these elements being predominant in the feeling. But fire can also be destructive and devastatingly powerful; if we dream of a burning house, fire symbolizes destructiveness not beauty.

Similar in some ways and different in others is the symbol of water—of the ocean or of a stream. Here, too, we find the blending of constant movement and yet of permanence. We also feel the quality of aliveness, continuity and energy. But there is a difference; where fire is adventurous, quick, exciting, water is quiet, slow and steady in a river or a lake. The ocean, however, can also be as destructive and unpredictable as fire.

The universal symbol is the only one in which the relationship between the symbol and that which is symbolizes is not coincidental but intrinsic. It is rooted in the experience of the affinity between an emotion or thought, on the one hand, and a sensory experience, on the other. It can be called universal because it is shared by all men, in contrast not only to the accidental symbol, which is by its very nature entirely personal, but also to the *conventional* symbol (as for instance a traffic signal), which is restricted to a group of people sharing the same convention. The universal symbol is rooted in the properties of our bodies, our senses and our minds, which are common to all men, and therefore not restricted to individuals or to specific groups. Indeed, the language of the universal symbol is the one common tongue developed by the human race.

For Freud, almost all symbols were accidental ones, with the one exception of sexual symbols; a tower or a stick is a symbol of male sexuality, and a house or the ocean, a symbol of female sexuality. In contrast to Jung, who thought all dreams are written in a clear and uncoded text, Freud thought exactly the opposite, that almost no dream could be understood without being decoded.

From my experience of interpreting many people's dreams, including my own, I believe that Freud, by dogmatic generalization, restricted the significance of his discovery of the censorship operating in a dream. There are many dreams in which the censorship consists of nothing but the poetic and symbolic language in which the content is expressed, but this is a "censorship" only for people with little poetic imagination. For those with a natural sense of poetry, the symbolic nature of the dream language can hardly be explained as censorship.

In the following I quote a dream (see Fromm, 1951a, chapter 6) which can be understood even without any association and where there are no elements of censorship. On the other hand, we can see that the associations brought up by the dreamer enrich our understanding of the dream:

A lawyer, twenty-eight years of age, wakes up and remembers the following dream which he later reports to the analyst: "I saw myself riding on a white charger, reviewing a large number of soldiers. They all cheered me wildly."

The first question the analyst asks his patient is rather general: "What comes to mind?" "Nothing," the man answers. "The dream is silly. You know that I dislike war and armies, that I certainly would not want to be a general." And in addition, "I also would not like to be the center of attention and to be stared at, cheering or no cheering, by thousands of soldiers. You know from what I told you about my professional problems how difficult it is for me even to plead a case in court with everybody looking at me."

The analyst answers: "Yes, but it does not do away with the fact that this is *your* dream, the plot *you* have written and in which you assigned yourself a role. In spite of all obvious inconsistencies, the dream must have some meaning and must make some sense. Let us begin with your associations to the dream contents. Focus on the dream picture, yourself and the white charger and the troops cheering—and tell me what comes to mind when you see this picture."

"Funny, I now see a picture which I used to like very much when I was fourteen or fifteen. It is a picture of Napoleon, yes indeed, on a white charger, riding in front of his troops. It is very similar to what I saw in the dream, except in that picture the soldiers did not cheer."

"This memory is certainly interesting. Tell me more about your liking for that picture and your interest in Napoleon."

"I can tell you a lot about it, but I find it embarrassing. Yes, when I was fourteen or fifteen I was rather shy. I was not very good in athletics and kind of afraid of tough kids. Oh, yes, now I remember an incident from that period which I had completely forgotten. I liked one of the tough kids very much and wanted to become his friend. We had hardly talked with each other, but I hoped that he would like me, too, if we would get better acquainted. One day— and it took a lot of courage—I approached him and asked him whether he would not like to come to my house; that I had a microscope and could show him a lot of interesting things. He looked at me for a moment, then he suddenly started to laugh and laugh and laugh. 'You sissy, why don't you invite some of your sisters' little friends?' I turned away, choking with tears. At that time I read voraciously about Napoleon; I collected pictures of him and indulged in daydreams of becoming like him, a famous general, admired by the whole world. Was he not small of stature, too? Was he not also a shy youngster like myself? Why could I not become like him? I spent many hours daydreaming; hardly ever concretely about the means to this end but always about the achievement. I *was* Napoleon, admired, envied, and yet magnanimous and ready to forgive my detractors. When I went to college I had got over my hero worship and my Napoleon daydreams; in fact I have not thought of this period for many years and certainly have never spoken to anyone about it. It kind of embarrasses me even now to talk to you about it."

" 'You' forgot about it, but the other you, that which determines many of your actions and feelings, well hidden from your daytime awareness, is still longing to be famous, admired, to have power. That other you spoke up in your dream last night; but let us see why just last night. Tell me what happened yesterday that was of importance to you."

"Nothing at all; it was a day like any other. I went to the office, worked to gather legal material for a brief, went home and had dinner, went to a movie and went to bed. That's all."

"That does not seem to explain why you rode on a white charger in the night. Tell me more about what went on at the office."

"Oh, I just remember . . . but this can't have anything to do with the dream . . . well, I'll tell you anyway. When I went to see my boss—the senior partner of the firm—for whom I collected the legal material, he discovered a mistake I had made. He looked at me critically and remarked, 'I am really surprised—I thought you would do better than that.' For the moment I was quite shocked —and the thought flashed through my mind that he would not take me into the firm as a partner later on as I had hoped he would. But I told myself that this was nonsense, that anyone could make a mistake, that he had just been irritable and that the episode had no bearing on my future. I forgot about the incident during the afternoon."

"How was your mood then? Were you nervous or kind of depressed?"

"No, not at all. On the contrary, I was just tired and sleepy. I found it difficult to work and was very glad when the time came to leave the office."

"The last thing of importance during that day, then, was your seeing the movie. Will you tell me what it was?"

"Yes, it was the film *Juarez,* which I enjoyed very much. In fact, I cried quite a bit."

"At what point?"

"First at the description of Juarez's poverty and suffering and then when he had been victorious; I hardly remember a movie which moved me so much."

"Then you went to bed, fell asleep, and saw yourself on the white charger, cheered by the troops. We understand a little better now why you had this dream, don't we? As a boy you felt shy, awkward, rejected. We know from our previous work that this had a great deal to do with your father, who was so proud of his success but so incapable of being close to you and of feeling—to say nothing of showing—affection and of giving encouragement. The incident you mentioned today, the rejection by the tough kid, was only the last straw, as it were. Your self-esteem had been badly damaged already, and this episode added one more element to make you certain that you could never be your father's equal, never amount to anything, that you would always be rejected by the people you admired. What could you do? You escaped into fantasy where you achieved the very things you felt incapable of achieving in real life. There, in the world of fantasy where nobody could enter and where nobody could disprove you, you were Napoleon, the great hero, admired by millions and—what is perhaps the most important thing—by yourself. As long as you could retain these fantasies you were protected from the acute pains that your feeling of inferiority caused you while you were in contact with the reality outside yourself. Then you went to college. You were less dependent on your father, felt some satisfaction in your studies, felt that you could make a new and better beginning. Moreover, you felt ashamed of your 'childish' daydreams, so you put them away; you felt you were on the way to being a real man. . . . But, as we have seen, this new confidence was somewhat deceptive. You were terribly frightened before every examination; you felt that no girl could really be interested in you if there was any other young man around; you were always afraid of your boss's criticism. This brings us to the day of the dream. The thing you tried so hard to avoid had happened—your boss had criticized you; you began to feel again the old feeling of inadequacy, but you pushed it away; you felt tired instead of feeling anxious and sad. Then you saw a movie which touched upon your old daydreams, the hero who became the admired savior of a nation after he had been the despised, powerless youngster. You pictured yourself, as you had done in your adolescence, as the hero, admired, cheered. Don't you see that you have not really given up the old retreat into fantasies of glory; that you have not burned the bridges that lead you back to that land of fantasy, but start to go back there whenever reality is disappointing and threatening? Don't you see that this fact, however, helps to create the very danger you are so afraid of, that of being childish, not an adult, not being taken seriously by grown-up men—and by yourself?"

The Relation of the Function of Sleeping to Dream Activity

Freud assumed that all dreams are essentially fulfillments of wishes and have the function of preserving our sleep by, as it were, hallucinatory fulfillment. After fifty years of interpreting dreams I must confess that I find this principle of Freud's only of limited validity. Undoubtedly he made a great discovery when he recognized that dreams are very often the symbolic satisfaction of wishes. But he damaged the significance of this discovery by the dogmatic assumption that this necessarily holds true for all dreams. Dreams can be wish fulfillments, dreams can express mere anxiety, but dreams can also—and this is the important point—express deep insights into oneself and into others. In order to appreciate this function of dreams, some consideration concerning the difference between the biological and psychological functions of sleeping and waking may be useful (see also Fromm, 1951a, chapter 3).

In the waking state thoughts and feelings respond primarily to challenge—the task of mastering our environment, changing it, defending ourselves against it. Survival is the task of waking man;

he is subject to the laws that govern reality. This means that he has to think in terms of time and space.

While we sleep we are not concerned with bending the outside world to our purposes. We are helpless, and sleep, therefore, has rightly been called the "brother of death." But we are also free, freer than when awake. We are free from the burden of work, from the task of attack or defense, from watching and mastering reality. We need not look at the outside world; we look at our inner world, are concerned exclusively with ourselves. When asleep we may be likened to a fetus or a corpse; we may also be likened to angels, who are not subject to the laws of "reality." In sleep the realm of necessity has given way to the realm of freedom in which "I am" is the only system to which thoughts and feelings refer.

Mental activity during sleep has a logic different from that of waking existence. As indicated before, sleep experience need not pay any attention to qualities that matter only when one copes with reality. If I feel, for instance, that a person is a coward, I may dream that he changed from a man into a chicken. This change makes sense in terms of what I feel about the person, not in terms of my orientation to outside reality.

Sleep and waking life are the two poles of human existence. Waking life is taken up with the function of action, sleep is freed from it. Sleep is taken up with the function of self-experience. When we wake from our sleep, we move into the realm of action. We are then oriented in terms of this system, and our memory operates within it; we remember what can be recalled in space-time concepts. The sleep world has disappeared. Experiences we had in it—our dreams—are remembered with the greatest difficulty.* The situation has been represented symbolically in many a folktale: at night ghosts and spirits, good and evil, occupy the

---

*On the problem of memory function in its relation to dream activity see the very stimulating article by E. Schachtel, *"Memory and Childhood Amnesia,"* (1947).

scene, but when dawn arrives, they disappear, and nothing is left of the intense experience.

Consciousness is the mental activity in our state of being preoccupied with external reality—with acting. (The qualities of consciousness are determined by the nature of action and by the survival function of the waking state of existence.) The unconscious is the mental experience in a state of existence in which we have shut off communications with the outer world, are no longer preoccupied with action but with our self-experience. The unconscious is an experience related to a special mode of life— that of nonactivity; and the characteristics of the unconscious follow from the nature of this mode of existence.

The "unconscious" is the unconscious only in relation to the "normal" state of activity. When we speak of "unconscious" we really say only that an experience is alien to that frame of mind which exists while we act; it is then felt as a ghostlike, intrusive element, hard to get hold of and hard to remember. But the day world is as unconscious in our sleep experience as the night world is in our waking experience. The term *unconscious* is customarily used solely from the standpoint of day experience; and thus it fails to denote that both conscious and unconscious are only different states of mind referring to different states of experience.

It will be argued that in the waking state of existence, too, thinking and feeling are not entirely subject to the limitations of time and space; that our creative imagination permits us to think about past and future objects as if they were present, and of distant objects as if they were before our eyes; that our waking feeling is not dependent on the physical presence of the object nor on its coexistence in time; that, therefore, the absence of the space-time system is not characteristic of sleep existence in contradistinction to waking existence, but of thinking and feeling in contradistinction to acting. This welcome objection permits me to clarify an essential point in my argument.

We must differentiate between the *contents* of thought processes and the *categories* employed in thinking. I can, for instance, think of my father and state that his attitude in a certain situation is identical with mine. This statement is rational. On the other hand, if I state, "I am my father," the statement is irrational because it is not conceived in reference to the physical world. The sentence is rational, however, in a purely experiential realm; it expresses the experience of identity with my father. Rational thought processes in the waking state are subject to categories which are rooted in a special form of existence—the one in which we relate ourselves to reality in terms of action. In my sleep existence, which is characterized by lack of even potential action, categories are employed which have reference only to my self-experience. The same holds true of feeling. Whatever I feel, in the waking state, with regard to a person whom I have not seen for twenty years, I remain aware that he or she is not present. If I dream about the person, my feeling deals with the person as if he or she were present. But to say "as if he were present" is to express the feeling in "waking life" concepts. In sleep existence there is no "as if"; the person *is* present.

In the foregoing pages the attempt has been made to describe the conditions of sleep and to draw from this description certain conclusions concerning the quality of dream activity. Does the understanding of dreams as fulfillments of wishes or as manifestations of feelings strong enough to be expressed even in our sleep exhaust the possible explanations of dreaming?

I would suggest that there is still another one, which is usually neglected. It is related to the fact that man has a deep need to explain to himself why he does or feels something. This is a generally observed and recognized fact, usually called rationalization. If we dislike somebody, for instance, we are not satisfied with carrying this feeling but we strive to make it appear as a reasonable consequence of certain facts; thus we endow the disliked person with qualities, real or often invented, which make our dislike appear to be reasonable.

The same of course holds true in the case of liking or admiring a person, and can be found in its most obvious form in the mass enthusiasm for certain leaders or the mass dislike for members of certain classes or races.

An example of posthypnotic phenomena is much to the point. Let us assume that somebody during a hypnotic trance receives the suggestion that he take off his coat five hours later, say at four o'clock in the afternoon, and forget that he has received this order. What happens at four o'clock? Although it may be cold he will take off his coat, but before or while doing so he will say something like this: "It is a particularly warm day today, quite out of season." He feels the necessity to explain to himself why he is doing what he does, and would indeed feel frightened to act without being able to explain why he does so.

Applying this principle to dreams, it might lead to the following hypothesis: that we feel in our sleep as we do in our waking life, but just as little as in the waking state can we tolerate having feelings which are not explained. Thus we invent a story which serves to explain why we feel fear or joy or hate, and so on. In other words, the dream has the function of rationalizing feelings which we experience during sleep. If that were so, it would indicate that even in our sleep we have the same tendency to make affects appear to be reasonable as we so clearly have in our waking life. Dreams thus can be looked at as the result of an inherent tendency to bend feelings to the requirements of reasonableness.

We must now proceed to study one specific element among the conditions of sleep which will prove to be of great significance in the understanding of dream processes. We have said that while we are asleep we are not occupied with managing outer reality. We do not perceive it and we do not influence it, nor are we subject to the influences of the outside world on us. From this it follows that the effect of this separation from reality depends on the quality of reality itself. If the influence from the outside world is essentially beneficial, the absence of this influence during sleep will tend to lower the value of our dream activity, so that it will be inferior to our mental activities during the daytime when we are exposed to the beneficial influence of outside reality.

But are we right in assuming that the influence of reality is mainly a beneficial one? May it not be that it is also harmful and that, therefore, the absence of its influence tends to bring forth qualities superior to those we have when we are awake?

In speaking of the reality outside ourselves, reference is not made primarily to the world of nature. Nature as such is neither good nor bad. It may be helpful to us or dangerous, and the absence of our perception of it relieves us, indeed, from our task of trying to master it or of defending ourselves against it; but it does not make us either more stupid or wiser, better or worse. It is quite different with the man-made world around us, with the culture in which we live. Its effect upon us is quite ambiguous, although we are prone to assume that it is entirely to our benefit.

Indeed, the evidence that cultural influences are beneficial to us seems almost overwhelming. What distinguishes us from the world of animals is our capacity to create culture.

Is, then, the man-made reality outside ourselves not the most significant factor in the development of the very best in us, and must we not expect that, when deprived of contact with the out-side world, we regress temporarily to a primitive, animal-like, unreasonable state of mind? Much can be said in favor of such an assumption, and the view that such a regression is the essential feature of the state of sleep, and thus of dream activity, has been held by many students of dreaming from Plato to Freud. From this viewpoint dreams are expected to be expressions of the irrational, primitive strivings in us, and the fact that we forget our dreams so easily is amply explained by our being ashamed of those irrational and criminal impulses which we express when we are not under the control of society. Undoubtedly to some extent, this interpretation of dreams is true, but the question is whether it is altogether true or whether the negative elements in the influence of society do not account for the paradox that *we are not only less reasonable and less decent in our dreams but that we are also more intelligent, wiser and capable of better judgment when we are asleep than when we are awake.*

Our dreams do not only express irrational desires but also deep insights and the important task of dream interpretation is to decide when the one and when the other is the case.

4. Freud's Instinct Theory and Its Critique

THE DEVELOPMENT OF THE INSTINCT THEORY

The last of Freud's great discoveries is his theory of the life and death instincts.*In 1920, with *Beyond the Pleasure Principle,* Freud began a fundamental revision of his whole theory of instincts. In this work Freud attributed to the "compulsion to repeat" the characteristics of an instinct; here, too, he postulated for the first time the new dichotomy of Eros and the death instinct, the nature of which he discussed in greater detail in *The Ego and the Id* (1923b) and in his further writings. This new dichotomy of life (Eros) and death instinct(s) took the place of the original dichotomy between ego and sexual instincts. Though Freud now attempted to identify Eros with libido, the new polarity constituted an entirely different concept of drive from the old one.

When Freud wrote *Beyond the Pleasure Principle* he was by no

*The following pages are taken from the appendix of Fromm (1973a).

means convinced that the new hypothesis was valid. "It may be asked," he wrote, "whether and how far I am myself convinced of the truth of the hypotheses that have been set out in these pages. My answer would be that I am not convinced myself and that I do not seek to persuade other people to believe in them. Or, more precisely, that I do not know how far I believe in them" (Freud, 1920g, p. 58f.). Considering that Freud was attempting to construct a new theoretical edifice, one which threatened the validity of many former concepts and which took a tremendous intellectual effort, his sincerity, which runs so shiningly through his whole work, is particularly impressive. He spent the next eighteen years working on the new theory, and increasingly acquired the sense of conviction he at first lacked. Not that he added entirely new aspects to the hypothesis; what he did, rather, was an intellectual "working through" that left him convinced, and must have made it all the more disappointing that not many of his own adherents really understood and shared his views. The new theory found its first full elaboration in *The Ego and the Id.* Of particular importance is the assumption about the

> special physiological process (of anabolism or catabolism) [which] would be associated with each of the two classes of instincts; both kinds of instinct would be active in every particle of living substance, though in unequal proportions, so that some one substance might be the principal representative of Eros. This hypothesis throws no light whatsoever upon the manner in which the two classes of instincts are fused, blended, and alloyed with each other; but that this takes place regularly and very extensively is an assumption indispensable to our conception. It appears that, as a result of the combination of unicellular organisms into multicellular forms of life, *the death instinct of the single cell* can successfully be neutralized and the *destructive impulses be diverted* on to the external world through the instrumentality of a special organ. This special organ would seem to be the muscular apparatus; and the death instinct would thus seem to express itself—though probably only in part—as an instinct of destruction directed against the external world and other organisms (Freud, 1923b, p. 41, italics added).

In these formulations Freud revealed the new direction of his thinking more explicitly than in *Beyond the Pleasure Principle*. Instead of the mechanistic physiologic approach of the older theory, which was built on the model of chemically produced tension and the need to reduce this tension to its normal threshold (pleasure principle), the approach of the new theory is a biological one in which each living cell is supposed to be endowed with the two basic qualities of living matter, Eros and the striving for death; however, the principle of tension reduction is preserved in a more radical form: the reduction of excitation to zero (Nirvana principle).

A year later (1924), in *Economic Problem of Masochism*, Freud took one further step in clarifying the relation between the two instincts. He wrote:

> The libido has the task of making the destroying instinct innocuous, and it fulfils the task by diverting that instinct to a great extent outwards—soon with the help of a special organic system, the muscular apparatus—towards objects in the external world. The instinct is then called the destructive instinct, the instinct for mastery, or the will to power.* A portion of the instinct is placed directly in the service of the sexual function, where it has an important part to play. This is sadism proper. Another portion does not share in this transposition outwards; it remains inside the organism and, with the help of the accompanying sexual excitation described above, becomes libidinally bound there. It is in this portion that we have to recognize the original, erotogenic masochism (Freud, 1924c, p. 163).

In the *New Introductory Lectures* (1933) the position taken earlier is maintained: Freud speaks of "the erotic instincts, which seek to combine more and more living substance into ever greater unities, and the death instincts, which oppose this effort and lead

---

*Freud combines here three very difficult tendencies. The instinct to destroy is basically different from the will for power: in the first case I want to destroy the object; in the second, I want to keep and control it—and both are entirely different from the drive for mastery, whose aim it is to create and produce, which in fact is the precise opposite of the will to destroy.—E.F.

what is living back into an inorganic state" (Freud, 1933a, p. 107). In the same lectures Freud wrote about the original destructive instinct:

> We can only perceive it under two conditions: if it is combined with erotic instincts into masochism or if—with a greater or lesser erotic addition—it is directed against the external world as aggressiveness. And now we are struck by the significance of the possibility that the aggressiveness may not be able to find satisfaction in the external world because it comes up against real obstacles. If this happens, it will perhaps retreat and increase the amount of self-destructiveness holding sway in the interior. We shall hear how this is in fact what occurs and how important a process this is. Impeded aggressiveness seems to involve a grave injury. *It really seems as though it is necessary for us to destroy some other thing or person in order not to destroy ourselves, in order to guard against the impulsion to self-destruction. A sad disclosure indeed for the moralist!*" (P. 105, italics added by E.F.)

In his last two papers, written one and two years before his death, Freud did not make any important alterations in the concepts as he had developed them in the foregoing years. In *Analysis Terminable and Interminable* (1937c) he emphasized even more the power of the death instinct. As James Strachey wrote in his editorial notes: "But the most powerful impeding factor of all *and one totally beyond any possibility of control . . . is the death instinct*" (1937c, p. 212, italics added). In *An Outline of Psychoanalysis* (written in 1938, published in 1940) Freud reaffirmed in a systematic way his earlier assumptions without making any relevant changes.

ANALYSIS OF THE INSTINCTIVISTIC ASSUMPTIONS

The foregoing brief description of Freud's new theories, that of Eros and of the death instinct, cannot show sufficiently how radical the change was from the old to the new theory, or that Freud did not see the radical nature of this change and as a consequence was stuck in many theoretical inconsistencies and immanent contradictions. In the following pages I shall attempt to describe the significance of the changes and to analyze the conflict between the old and the new theory.

Freud, after the First World War, had two new visions. The first was that of the power and intensity of aggressive-destructive strivings in man, independent of sexuality. Saying that this was a *new* vision is not entirely correct. As I have already shown, he had not been entirely unaware of the existence of aggressive impulses independent of sexuality. But this insight was expressed only sporadically, and it never changed the main hypothesis about the basic polarity between sexual instincts and ego instincts, even though this theory was later modified by the introduction of the concept of narcissism. In the theory of the death instinct the awareness of human destructiveness bursts forth in full strength, and destructiveness becomes the one pole of existence which, fighting with the other pole, Eros, forms the very essence of life. Destructiveness becomes a *primary* phenomenon of life.

The second vision that marks Freud's new theory is not only without antecedents in his former theory, but is in full contradiction to it. It is the vision that Eros, present in every cell of living substance, has as its aim the unification and integration of all cells, and beyond that, the service of civilization, the integration of smaller units into the unity of mankind (Freud, 1930a). Freud discovers nonsexual love. He calls the life instinct also "love instinct"; love is identified with life and growth, and—fighting with the death instinct—it determines human existence. In Freud's older theory man was looked upon as an isolated system, driven by two impulses: one to survive (ego instinct) and one to have pleasure by overcoming the tensions that in turn were chemically produced within the body and localized in the "erogenous zones," of which the genitals were one. In this picture man was primarily isolated, but entered into relations with members of the other sex in order to satisfy his striving for pleasure. The relationship between the two sexes was conceived in a way that resembles human relations in the marketplace. Each is only concerned with the satisfaction of his needs, but it is precisely for the sake of this satisfaction that he has to enter into relations with others who offer what he needs, and need what he offers.

In the Eros theory this is entirely different. Man is no longer conceived of as primarily isolated and egotistical, as *l'homme machine,* but as being primarily related to others, impelled by the life instincts which make him need union with others. Life, love and growth are one and the same, more deeply rooted and fundamental than sexuality and "pleasure."

The change in Freud's vision shows clearly in his new evaluation of the biblical commandment "Thou shalt love thy neighbor as thyself." In *Why War?* (1933b) he wrote:

> Anything that encourages the growth of emotional ties between men must operate against war. These ties may be of two kinds. In the first place they may be relations resembling those toward a loved object, though *without having a sexual aim.* There is no need for psychoanalysis to be ashamed to speak of love in this connection, for religion itself uses the same words: "Thou shalt love thy neighbor as thyself." This, however, is more easily said than done. The second kind of emotional tie is by means of identification. Whatever leads men to share important interests produces this community of feeling, these identifications. And the structure of human society is to a large extent based on them (p. 212, italics added).

These lines are written by the same man who only three years earlier had ended a comment on this same biblical commandment by asking: "What is the point of a precept enunciated with so much solemnity if its fulfillment *cannot be recommended as reasonable?*" (Freud, 1930a, p. 110, italics added by E.F.)

Nothing short of a radical change of viewpoint had occurred. Freud, the enemy of religion, which he had called an illusion preventing man from reaching maturity and independence, now quotes one of the most fundamental commandments to be found in all great humanistic religions, in support of his psychological assumption. He emphasizes that there is "no need for psycho-

analysis to be ashamed to speak of love in this connection"
(Freud, 1933b, p. 212, cf., 1908d), but, indeed, he needs this
assertion to overcome the embarrassment he must have felt in
making this drastic change with regard to the concept of broth-
erly love.

Was Freud aware how drastic the change in his approach was?
Was he conscious of the profound and irreconcilable contradiction between the old and the new theories? Quite obviously he
was not. In *The Ego and the Id* (1923b) he identified Eros (life
instinct or love instinct) with the sexual instincts (plus the instinct
for self-preservation):

> According to this view we have to distinguish two classes of in-
> stincts, one of which, *the sexual instincts or Eros,* is by far the more
> conspicuous and accessible to study. It comprises not merely the
> uninhibited sexual instinct proper and the instinctual impulses of
> an aim-inhibited or sublimated nature derived from it, but also the
> self-preservative instinct, which must be assigned to the ego and
> which at the beginning of our analytic work we had good reason
> for contrasting with the sexual object-instincts (p. 40, italics
> added).

It is precisely because of his unawareness of the contradiction
that he made the attempt to reconcile the old and the new theories in such a way that they seemed to form a continuity without
a sharp break. This attempt had to lead to many immanent contradictions and inconsistencies in the new theory, which Freud
again and again tried to bridge, smooth over or deny, yet without
ever succeeding in doing so. In the following pages I shall attempt to describe the vicissitudes of the new theory produced by
Freud's failure to recognize that the new wine—and in this case,
I believe, the better wine—could not be put into the old bottles.

Before we start this analysis still another change must be mentioned which, also unrecognized by Freud, complicated matters
still more. Freud had built his older theory on a scientific model
that is easy to recognize: the mechanistic-materialistic model that
had been the scientific ideal of his teacher von Brücke and the

entire circle of mechanistic-materialists including Helmholtz and Büchner.* They looked on man as a machine driven by chemical processes: feelings, affects and emotions were explained as being caused by specific and identifiable physiological processes. Most of hormonology and of the neurophysiological findings of the last decades were unknown to these men, yet with daring and ingenuity they insisted on the correctness of their approach. Needs and interests for which no somatic sources could be found were ignored, and the understanding of those processes which were not neglected followed the principles of mechanistic thinking. The model of von Brücke's physiology and Freud's model of man could be repeated today in a properly programmed computer. "He" develops a certain amount of tension which at a certain threshold has to be relieved and reduced, while this realization is checked by another part, the ego, which observes reality and inhibits relief when it conflicts with the needs for survival. This Freudian robot would be similar to Isaac Asimov's science-fiction robot, but the programming would be different. Its first law would not be not to hurt human beings, but to avoid self-damage or self-destruction.

The new theory does not follow this mechanistic "physiologizing" model. It is centered on a biological orientation in which the fundamental forces of life (and its opposite: death) become the primal forces motivating man. The nature of the cell—that is, of all living substance—becomes the theoretical basis for a theory of motivation, not a physiological process that goes on in certain

---

*The dependence of Freud's theory formation on the thinking of his teachers has been described by Peter Ammacher (1962). Robert R. Holt (1965, p. 94) summarizes approvingly the main thesis of Ammacher's work in the following: "Many of the most puzzling and seemingly arbitrary turns of psychoanalytic theory, involving propositions that are false to the extent that they are testable at all, are either hidden biological assumptions or result directly from such assumptions, which Freud learned from his teachers in medical school. They became a basic part of his intellectual equipment, as unquestioned as the assumption of the universal determinism, were probably not always recognized by him as biological, and thus were retained as necessary ingredients when he attempted to turn away from neurologizing to the construction of an abstract, psychological model."

organs of the body. The new theory was perhaps closer to a vitalistic philosophy (see Pratt, 1958) than to the concept of the German mechanistic materialists. But, as I already said, Freud was not clearly aware of this change; hence he tries again and again to apply his physiologizing method to the new theory and necessarily has to fail in this attempt to square the circle. However, in one important regard both theories have a common premise which has been the unchanged axiom of Freud's thinking: the concept that the governing law of the psychic apparatus is the tendency to reduce tension (or excitation) to a constant low level (the constancy principle—upon which the pleasure principle rests), or to the zero level (the Nirvana principle, upon which the death instinct is based).

We must now return to a more detailed analysis of Freud's two new visions, that of the death instinct and of the life instinct, as the primal determining forces of human existence.*

What motivated Freud to postulate the death instinct?

One factor which I have already mentioned was probably the impact of the First World War. He, like many other men of his time and age, had shared the optimistic vision so characteristic of the European middle class, and saw himself suddenly confronted with a fury of hate and destruction hardly believable before August 1, 1914.

One might speculate that to this historical factor a personal factor could be added. As we know from Ernest Jones's biography, Freud was a man preoccupied with death. He thought of dying every day, after he was forty; he had attacks of *Todesangst* ("fear of death"), and sometimes he would add to his "goodbye": "You might never see me again" (Jones, 1957, p. 301). One might surmise that Freud's severe illness would have impressed

---

*Freud's terminology is not always consistent. He speaks sometimes of life and death instincts, sometimes of a life and death instinct (singular). The death instinct(s) is also called destructive instinct(s). The word *thanatos* (parallel to Eros), as an equivalent to death instinct, was not used by Freud, but was introduced into the discussion by P. Federn.

him as a confirmation of his fear of death, and thus contributed to the formulation of the death instinct. This speculation, however, is untenable in this simplified form, since the first signs of his illness did not appear until February 1923, several years after his conception of the death instinct. But it might be not too farfetched to assume that his earlier preoccupation with death grew in intensity as he became sick, and led him to a concept in which the conflict between life and death was at the center of human experience, rather than the conflict between the two life-affirmative drives, sexual desire and ego drives. To assume that man needs to die because death is the hidden goal of his life might be considered a kind of comfort destined to alleviate his fear of death.

While these historical and personal factors constitute one set of motivations for Freud's construction of the death instinct, there is another set of factors which must have inclined him to conceive of this theory. Freud always thought in dualistic terms. He saw opposite forces battling each other, and the life process as the outcome of this battle. Sex and the drive for self-preservation was the original form assumed by the dualistic theory. But with the concept of narcissism which put the self-preservative instinct in the camp of the libido, the old dualism seemed to be threatened. Did the theory of narcissism not impose a monistic theory that all instincts were libidinous? And even worse, would that not justify one of the main heresies of Jung, the concept of libido as denoting *all psychic energy?* Indeed, Freud had to extricate himself from this intolerable dilemma, intolerable because it would have amounted to agreeing with Jung's concept of libido. He had to find a new instinct, opposed to the libido, as the basis for a new dualistic approach. The death instinct fulfilled this requirement. To replace the old dualism, a new one had been found, and existence could be viewed again dualistically as the battlefield of opposing instincts, Eros and the death instinct.

In the case of the new dualism Freud followed a pattern of thinking, about which more will be said later, and constructed two broad concepts into which every phenomenon had to fit. He had done that with the concept of sexuality by enlarging it, so that everything that was not ego instinct belonged to the sexual instinct. He followed the same method again with the death instinct. He made it so broad that as a result every striving which was not subsumed under Eros belonged to the death instinct, and vice versa. In this way aggressiveness, destructiveness, sadism, the drive for control and mastery were, in spite of their qualitative differences, manifestations of the same force—the death instinct.

In still another aspect Freud followed the same pattern of thinking that had had such a strong hold over him in the earlier phase of his theoretical system. About the death instinct he says that it is originally all inside; then part of it is sent outwards and acts as aggressiveness, while part of it remains in the interior as primary masochism. But when the part that is sent outwards meets with obstacles too great to overcome, the death instinct is redirected inward and manifests itself as secondary masochism. This pattern of reasoning is exactly the same as that employed by Freud in his discussion of narcissism. At first all libido is in the ego (primary narcissism), then it is extended outward to objects (object libido), but it is often directed again to the interior and then forms the so-called secondary narcissism.

Many times "death instinct" is used synonymously with "instinct of destruction" and "aggressive instincts" (see for instance Freud, 1930a). But at the same time, Freud makes fine distinctions between these different terms. By and large, as James Strachey has pointed out in his introduction to *Civilization and Its Discontents* (Freud, 1930a), in Freud's later writings—for instance *Civilization and Its Discontents, The Ego and the Id* (1923b), *New Introductory Lectures* (1933a), *An Outline of Psychoanalysis* (1940a)—the aggressive instinct is something secondary, derived from the primary self-destruction.

Here are some examples of this relationship between the death instinct and aggressiveness. In *Civilization and Its Discontents* Freud writes that the death instinct is "diverted towards the external world and comes to light as an instinct of aggressiveness and destructiveness" (Freud, 1930a, p. 118). In the *New Introductory Lectures* he speaks of "self-destructiveness *as an expression* of a 'death instinct' which cannot fail to be present in every vital process" (Freud, 1933a, p. 107, italics added). In the same work Freud makes this thought still more explicit: "We are led to the view that masochism is older than sadism, and that sadism is the destructive instinct directed outwards, thus acquiring the characteristic of aggressiveness" (p. 105). The amount of destructive instinct which remains in the interior either combines "with erotic instincts into masochism or—with a greater or lesser erotic addition—it is directed against the external world as aggressiveness." But, so continues Freud, if the aggressiveness directed outward meets with obstacles that are too strong it returns and increases the amount of self-destructiveness holding sway in the interior (ibid.). The end of this theoretical and somewhat contradictory development is reached in Freud's last two papers. In the *Outline* he says that within the id "the organic *instincts* operate which are themselves compounded of fusions of *two primal forces* (Eros and Destructiveness) in varying proportions . . ." (Freud, 1940a, p. 198, italics added). In *Analysis Terminable and Interminable* Freud also speaks of the death instinct and Eros as two "primal instincts" (Freud, 1937c).

It is amazing and impressive how firmly Freud stuck to his concept of the death instinct, in spite of great theoretical difficulties that he tried hard—and in my opinion, vainly—to overcome.

The main difficulty perhaps lies in the assumption of the identity of two tendencies, that of the body's tendency to return to the original, inorganic state (as an outcome of the principle of repetition compulsion) and that of the instinct to destroy, either oneself or others. For the first tendency the term *thanatos,* referring to death, may be adequate, or even "Nirvana principle," indicating the tendency to the reduction of *tension,* of energy, to the point of the end of all energetic strivings.* But is this slow decrease of life force the same as destructiveness? Of course, logically it could be argued—and Freud implicitly does so—that if a tendency toward dying is inherent in the organism, there must be an active force that tends to destroy. (This is really the same kind of thinking that we find among the instinctivists who postulate a special instinct behind every kind of behavior.) But if we go beyond such circular reasoning, is there any evidence or even reason for this identity of the tendency toward cessation of all excitation and the impulse to destroy? It hardly seems so. If we assume, following Freud's reasoning on the basis of the repetition compulsion, that life has an inherent tendency toward slowing down and eventually dying, such a biologically innate tendency would be quite different from the active impulse to destroy. If we add that this same tendency to die is also supposed to be the source of the passion for power and the instinct for mastery, and —when mixed with sexuality—the source of sadism and masochism, the theoretical tour de force must end in failure. The "Nirvana principle" and the passion for destruction are two disparate entities that cannot be brought under the same category of death instinct(s).

A further difficulty lies in the fact that the death "instinct" does not fit Freud's general concept of instincts. First of all it does not have, as do the instincts in Freud's earlier theory, a special zone in the body from which it originates, rather it is a biological force inherent in all living substance. This point has been made convincingly by Otto Fenichel:

> Dissimulation in the cells . . .—that is to say an objective destruc-
> tion—cannot be the source of a destructive instinct in the same

*The use of "Nirvana principle" is unfortunate inasmuch as it misinterprets the Buddhist Nirvana. Nirvana is precisely not a state of lifelessness brought about by nature (which, according to Buddhism, has the opposite tendency), but by the spiritual effort of man who finds salvation and the completion of life if he has succeeded in overcoming all greed and egoism and is filled with compassion for all sentient beings. In the state of Nirvana the Buddha experienced supreme joy.

sense that a chemically determined sensitization of the central organ through stimulation of the erotogenetic zones is the source of the sexual instinct. For according to the definition, instinct aims at *eliminating* the somatic change which we designate as the source of the instinct: but the death instinct does not aim at eliminating dissimulation. For this reason it does not seem to me possible to set up the "death instinct" as one species of instinct over against another species (Fenichel, 1945, p. 60f.).

Fenichel points here to one of the theoretical difficulties Freud created for himself, even though, as we may say, he repressed the awareness of it. This difficulty is all the more serious since Freud, as I shall show later, had to come to the conclusion that Eros does not fulfill the theoretical conditions of an instinct either. Certainly, had Freud not had strong personal motivations, he would not have used the term *instinct* in a completely different sense from the original one without pointing out this difference himself. (This difficulty makes itself felt even in the terminology. Eros cannot be used together with "instinct" and logically Freud never talked about an "eros instinct." But he made a place for the term *instinct* by using "life instinct" alternatively with Eros.)

Actually, the death instinct has no connection with Freud's earlier theory, except in the general axiom of drive reduction. As we have seen, in the earlier theory aggression was either a component drive of pregenital sexuality or an ego drive directed against stimuli from the outside. In the theory of the death instinct no connection is made with the former sources of aggression, except that the death instinct, when mixed with sexuality, is now used to explain sadism (Freud, 1933a, p. 104f.).

To sum up, the concept of the death instinct was determined by two main requisites: first, by the need to accommodate Freud's new conviction of the power of human aggression; second, by the need to stick to a dualistic concept of instincts. After the ego instincts had also been considered to be libidinous, Freud had to find a new dichotomy, and the one between Eros and the death instinct offered itself as the most convenient one. But while convenient from the standpoint of immediately solving a problem, it was very inconvenient from the standpoint of the development of Freud's whole theory of instinctual motivation. The death instinct became a "catchall" concept, by the use of which one tried without success to resolve incompatible contradictions. Freud, perhaps due to his age and illness, did not approach the problem squarely and thus patched up the contradictions. Most of the psychoanalysts who did not accept his concept of Eros and death instinct found an easy solution; they transformed the death instinct into a "destructive instinct" opposite of the old sexual instinct. They thus combined their loyalty to Freud with their inability to go beyond the old-fashioned instinct theory. Even considering the difficulties of the new theory, it constituted a considerable achievement: it recognized as the basic conflict of human existence the choice between life and death, and it relinquished the old physiological concept of drives for a more profound biological speculation. Freud did not have the satisfaction of finding a solution, and he had to leave his instinct theory as a torso. The further development of his theory must face the problem and deal squarely with the difficulties, hoping to find new solutions.

In discussing the theory of the *life instinct* and of Eros, we find that the theoretical difficulties are, if anything, even more serious than those connected with the concept of the death instinct. The reason for the difficulties is obvious. In the libido theory the excitation was due to the chemically determined sensitization, through the stimulation of the various erotogenic zones. In the case of the life instinct we are dealing with a tendency, characteristic of all living substance, of which there is no specific physiological source or specific organ. How could the old sexual instinct and the new life instinct—how could sexuality and Eros—be the same?

Yet, although Freud wrote in the *New Introductory Lectures* that the new theory had "replaced" the libido theory, he affirmed in the same lectures and elsewhere that the sexual instincts and Eros are identical. He wrote: "Our hypothesis is that there are two essentially different classes of instincts: the sexual instincts, understood in the widest sense—Eros, if you prefer that name—and the aggressive instincts, whose aim is destruction" (Freud, 1933a, p. 103). Or, in *An Outline of Pyschoanalysis:* "The total available energy of Eros . . . henceforth we shall speak of as 'libido' " (Freud, 1940a, p. 150). Sometimes he identifies Eros with the sexual instinct *and* the instinct for self-preservation (Freud, 1923b), which was only logical after he had revised the original theory and classified both the original enemies, the self-preservative and the sexual instincts, as being libidinous. But while Freud sometimes equates Eros and libido, he expresses a slightly different viewpoint in his last work, *An Outline of Psychoanalysis.* Here he writes: "The greater part of what we know about Eros—that is to say, about its exponent, the libido—has been gained from a study of the sexual function, which, indeed, on the prevailing view, *even if not according to our theory,* coincides with Eros" (Freud, 1940a, p. 151, italics added). According to this statement, and in contradiction to those quoted before, Eros and sexuality do *not* coincide. It seems that what Freud has in mind here is that Eros is a "primal instinct" (aside from the death instinct), of which the sexual instinct is *one exponent.* In fact, he returns here to a view expressed already in *Beyond the Pleasure Principle* where he says in a footnote that the sexual instinct "was transformed for us into Eros, which seeks to force together and hold together the portions of living substance. What are commonly called the sexual instincts are looked upon by us as the part of Eros which is directed towards objects" (Freud, 1920g, p. 61).

Once Freud even makes the attempt to indicate that his original concept of sexuality "was by no means identical with the impulsion towards a union of the two sexes or towards producing a pleasurable sensation in the genitals; it had far more resemblance to the all-inclusive and all-preserving Eros of Plato's *Sym-*

posium" (Freud, 1925e, p. 218). The truth of the first part of this statement is obvious. Freud had always defined sexuality as broader than genital sexuality. But it is difficult to see on what basis he maintains that his older concept of sexuality resembled that of the Platonic Eros.

The older sexual theory was precisely the opposite of the Platonic theory. The libido was male according to Freud, and there was no corresponding female libido. The woman, in line with Freud's extreme patriarchal bias, was not man's equal but a crippled, castrated male. The very essence of the Platonic myth is that male and female were once one and were then divided into halves, which implies, of course, that the two halves are equals, that they form a polarity endowed with the tendency to unite again.

The only reason for Freud's attempt to interpret the old libido theory in the light of Plato's Eros must have been his wish to deny the discontinuity of the two phases, even at the expense of an obvious distortion of his older theory.

As in the case of the death instinct, Freud ran into a difficulty with regard to the instinctual nature of the life instinct. As Fenichel (1945) has pointed out, the death instinct cannot be called an "instinct" in terms of Freud's *new* concept of instinct, developed first in *Beyond the Pleasure Principle* and continued throughout his later work, including the *Outline of Psychoanalysis.* Freud wrote: "Though they [the instincts] are the ultimate cause of all activity, they are of a conservative nature; the state whatever it may be, which an organism has reached, gives rise to a tendency to reestablish that state as soon as it has been abandoned" (Freud, 1940a, p. 148).

Have Eros and the life instinct this conservative quality of all instincts, and thus can they be properly called an instinct? Freud was trying hard to find a solution that would save the conservative character of the life instincts.

In speaking of the germ cells that "work against the death of the living substance and succeed in winning for it what we can only regard as potential immortality" (Freud, 1920g, p. 40), he stated:

> The instincts which watch over the destinies of these elementary organisms that survive the whole individual, which provide them with a safe shelter while they are defenseless against the stimuli of the external world, which bring about their meeting with other germ cells, and so on—these constitute the group of the sexual instincts. They are conservative in the same sense as the other instincts in that they bring back earlier states of living substance; but they are conservative to a higher degree in that they are peculiarly resistant to external influences; and they are conservative too in another sense in that they preserve life itself for a comparatively long period. They are the true life instincts. They operate against the purpose of the other instincts, which leads, by reason of their function, to death; and this fact indicates that there is an opposition between them and the other instincts, an opposition whose importance was long ago recognized by the theory of the neuroses. It is as though the life of the organism moved with a vacillating rhythm. One group of instincts rushes forward so as to reach the final aim of life as swiftly as possible; but when a particular stage in the advance has been reached, the other group jerks back to a certain point to make a fresh start and so prolong the journey. And even though it is certain that sexuality *and the distinction between the sexes did not exist when life began,* the possibility remains that the instincts which were later to be described as sexual may have been in operation from the very first, and it may not be true that it was only at a later time that they started upon their work of opposing the activities of the "ego instincts" (Freud, 1920g, p. 41, italics added by E.F.).

What is most interesting in this passage, and the reason I quote it at length, is how almost desperately Freud tried to save the conservative concept of all instincts and hence also of the life instinct. He had to take refuge in a new formulation of the sexual instinct as one that watches over the destinies of the germ cell, a definition different from his whole concept of instinct in his previous work.

A few years later, in *The Ego and the Id* Freud made the attempt to give Eros the status of a true instinct, by ascribing to it a conservative nature. He wrote:

> On the basis of theoretical considerations, supported by biology, we put forward the hypothesis of a death instinct, the task of which is to lead organic life back into the inanimate state; on the other hand, we supposed that Eros, by bringing about a more and more far-reaching combination of the particles into which living substance is dispersed, aims at complicating life and at the same time, of course, at preserving it. Acting in this way, both the instincts would be conservative in the strictest sense of the word, since both would be endeavouring to re-establish a state of things that was disturbed by the emergence of life. The emergence of life would thus be the cause of the continuance of life and also at the same time of the striving towards death; and life itself would be a conflict and compromise between these two trends. The problem of the origin of life would remain a cosmological one; and the problem of the goal and purpose of life would be answered dualistically (Freud, 1923b, p. 40).

Eros aims at complicating life and preserving it, and hence is also conservative, because with the emergence of life an instinct is born which is to preserve it. But, we must ask, if it is the nature of the instinct to re-establish the earliest state of existence, inorganic matter, how can it at the same time tend to re-establish a later form of existence, namely life?

After these futile attempts to save the conservative character of the life instinct, Freud, in the *Outline*, finally arrives at a negative solution: "In the case of Eros (and the love instinct) we *cannot* apply this formula [of the conservative character of the instincts]. To do so would presuppose that living substance was once a unity which had later been torn apart and was now striving towards re-union" (Freud, 1940a, p. 149, italics added). Freud adds here a significant footnote: "Certain writers have imagined something of the sort, but nothing like it is known to us from the actual history of living substance" (ibid.). Quite obviously Freud refers here to Plato's Eros myth, yet he objects to it as a product of poetic imagination. This rejection is truly puzzling. The Platonic answer would indeed satisfy the theoretical requirement of the conservative nature of Eros. What could be more fitting to accommodate the formula that the instinct tends to restore an earlier situation than that male and female were unified in the beginning, then separated, and were driven by the wish for reunion? Why did Freud not accept this way out and thus rid himself of the theoretical embarrassment that Eros was not a true instinct?

Perhaps some more light is thrown on this question if we compare this footnote in the *Outline* with a much more detailed and earlier statement in *Beyond the Pleasure Principle*. Here he quoted Plato's report in the *Symposium* concerning the original unity of man who was then divided into halves by Zeus, and after this division, each desiring his other half, they came together and threw their arms about one another eager to grow into one. He wrote:

> Shall we follow the hint given us by the poet-philosopher, and venture upon the hypothesis that living substance at the same time of its coming to life was torn apart into small particles, which have ever since endeavoured to reunite through the sexual instincts? That these instincts, in which the chemical affinity of inanimate matter persisted, gradually succeeded, as they developed through the kingdom of the protista, in overcoming the difficulties put in the way of that endeavour by an environment charged with dangerous stimuli—stimuli which compelled them to form a protective cortical layer? That these splintered fragments of living substance in this way attained a multicellular condition and finally transferred the instinct for reuniting, in the most highly concentrated form, to the germ cells?—But here, I think, the moment has come for breaking off" (Freud, 1920g, p. 58).

We easily see the difference between the two statements: in the earlier formulation *(Beyond the Pleasure Principle)* Freud leaves the answer open, while in the later statement *(An Outline of Psychoanalysis)* the answer is definitely negative.

But much more important is the particular formulation that is common to both statements. Both times he speaks of "living substance" having been torn apart. The Platonic myth, however, does not speak of "living substance" having been torn apart, but of *male* and *female* having been torn apart and striving to be reunited. Why did Freud insist on "living substance" as the crucial point?

I believe the answer may lie in a subjective factor. Freud was deeply imbued with the patriarchal feeling that men are superior to women, and not their equals. Hence the theory of a male-female polarity—which like all polarity implies difference *and* equality—was unacceptable to him. This emotional male bias had, at a much earlier period, led him to the theory that women are crippled men, governed by the castration complex and penis envy, inferior to men also by the fact that their superego is weaker, their narcissism, however, stronger than that of men. While one can admire the brilliance of his construction, it is hard to deny that the assumption that one-half of the human race is a crippled version of the other half is nothing short of an absurdity, only explainable by the depth of sex prejudice (not too different from racial prejudice and/or religious prejudice). Is it surprising, then, that Freud was blocked here, too, when by following Plato's myth he would have been forced into an assumption of male-female equality? Indeed, Freud could not take this step; thus he changed male-female union to union of "living substance" and rejected the logical way out of the difficulty that Eros did not partake in the conservative nature of instincts.

Critique of Freud's Instinct Theory

Freud was a prisoner of the feelings and thought habits of his society, which he was unable to transcend. When a new vision struck him, only part of it—or its consequences—became conscious, while another part remained unconscious because it was incompatible with his "complex" and previous conscious thought. His conscious thinking had to try to deny the contradictions and inconsistencies by making constructions that were sufficiently plausible to satisfy conscious thought processes.

Freud did not and—as I have tried to show—could not choose the solution of making Eros fit his own definition of instincts—that is, fit their conservative nature. Was there another theoretical option open to him? I believe there was. He could have found another solution to accommodate his new vision, the dominant role of love and of destructiveness, within his old traditional libido theory. He could have set up a polarity between *pregenital sexuality* (oral and anal sadism) as the source of destructiveness and *genital sexuality* as the source of love. But of course this solution was difficult for Freud to accept for a reason mentioned before in another context. It would have come dangerously close to a monistic view, because both destructiveness *and* love would have been libidinous. Yet, Freud had already laid the basis for connecting destructiveness with pregenital sexuality by arriving at the conclusion that the destructive part of the anal-sadistic libido is the death instinct (Freud, 1923b, 1920g). If that is so, it seems fair to speculate that the anal libido itself must have a deep affinity to the death instinct; in fact the further conclusion might seem warranted that it is of the essence of the anal libido to aim for destruction.

But Freud does not come to this conclusion, and it is interesting to speculate why he did not.

The first reason lies in too narrow an interpretation of the anal libido. For Freud and his pupils the essential aspect of anality lies in the tendency to control and possess (aside from a friendly aspect of retaining). Now, controlling and possessing are certainly tendencies opposite of loving, furthering, liberating, which form a syndrome among themselves. But "possession" and "control" do not contain the very essence of destructiveness, the wish to destroy, and hostility toward life. No doubt, the anal character has a deep interest in and affinity to feces as part of their general affinity to all that is not alive. Feces are the product finally eliminated by the body, being of no further use to it. The anal character is attracted by feces as he is attracted by everything that is useless for life, such as dirt, death, decay. We can say that the tendency to control and possess is only one aspect of the anal character, but milder and less malignant than hatred of life. I believe that had Freud seen this direct connection between feces and death he might have arrived at the conclusion that the main polarity is that between the genital and the anal orientations, two clinically well-studied entities that are the equivalents of Eros and of the death instinct. Had he done so, Eros and the death instinct would not have appeared as two biologically given and equally strong tendencies, but Eros would have been looked upon as the biologically normal aim of development, while the death instinct would have been seen to be based on a failure of normal development and in this sense a pathological, though deeply rooted, striving. If one wants to entertain a biological speculation one might relate anality to the fact that orientation by smell is characteristic of all four-legged mammals, and that the erect posture implies the change from orientation by smell to orientation by sight. The change in function of the old olfactory brain would correspond to the same transformation of orientation. In view of this, one might consider that the anal character constitutes a regressive phase of biological development for which there might even be a constitutional-genetic basis. The anality of the infant could be considered as representing an evolutionary repetition of a biologically earlier phase in the process of transition to fully developed human functioning. (In Freud's terms, anality-destructiveness would have the conservative nature of an instinct, i.e., the return from genitality-love-sight orientation to anality-destruction-smell orientation.)

The relationship between death instinct and life instinct would have been essentially the same as that between pregenital and genital libido in Freud's developmental scheme. The libido fixation on the anal level would have been a pathological phenomenon, but one with deep roots in the psychosexual constitution, while the genital level would be characteristic of the healthy individual. In this speculation, then, the anal level would have two rather different aspects: one, the drive to control; the other, the drive to destroy. As I have attempted to show, this would be the difference between sadism and necrophilia.

But Freud did not make this connection, and perhaps could not make it for the reasons that have been discussed earlier in connection with the difficulties in the theory of Eros.

In the previous pages I have pointed to the immanent contradictions into which Freud was forced when he changed from the libido theory to the Eros–death-instinct theory. There is another conflict of a different kind in the latter theory which must attract our attention: the conflict between Freud the theoretician and Freud the humanist. The theoretician arrives at the conclusion that man has only the alternative between destroying himself (slowly, by illness) or destroying others; or—putting it in other words—between causing suffering either to himself or to others. The humanist rebels against the idea of this tragic alternative that would make war a rational solution of this aspect of human existence.

Not that Freud was averse to tragic alternatives. On the contrary, in his earlier theory he had constructed such a tragic alternative: repression of instinctual demands (especially pregenital ones) was supposed to be the basis of the development of civilization: the repressed instinctual drive was "sublimated" into valuable cultural channels, but still at the expense of full human happiness. On the other hand, repression led not only to increasing civilization but also to the development of neurosis among the many in whom the repressive process did not work successfully. Lack of civilization combined with full happiness or civilization combined with neurosis and diminished happiness seemed to be the alternative.

The contradiction between the death instinct and Eros confronts man with a real and truly tragic alternative, a real alternative because he can decide to attack and wage war, to be aggressive, and to express his hostility because he prefers to do this rather than to be sick. That this alternative is a tragic one hardly needs to be proven, at least not as far as Freud or any other humanist is concerned.

Freud makes no attempt to befog the issue by blurring the sharpness of the conflict. As quoted earlier, in the *New Introductory Lectures* he wrote: "And now we are struck by the significance of the possibility that the aggressiveness may not be able to find satisfaction in the external world because it comes up against real obstacles. If this happens, it will perhaps retreat and increase the amount of self-destructiveness holding sway in the interior. We shall hear how this is in fact what occurs and how important a process this is" (Freud, 1933a, p. 105).

In *An Outline of Psychoanalysis* he wrote: "Holding back aggressiveness is in general unhealthy and leads to illness" (Freud, 1940a, p. 150). After having thus drawn the lines sharply, how does Freud respond to the impulse not to view human affairs so hopelessly and to avoid siding with those who recommend war as the best medicine for the human race?

Indeed, Freud made several theoretical attempts to find a way out of the dilemma between the theoretician and the humanist. One attempt lay in the idea that the destructive instinct can be transformed into conscience. In *Civilization and Its Discontents* Freud asks: "What happens to him [the aggressor] to render his desire for aggression innocuous?" Freud answers thus:

> Something very remarkable, which we should never have guessed and which is nevertheless quite obvious. His aggressiveness is introjected, internalized; it is, in point of fact, sent back to where it came from—that is, it is directed towards his own ego. There it is taken over by a portion of the ego which sets itself over against the rest of the ego as super-ego, and which now, in the form of "conscience," is ready to put into action against the ego the same harsh aggressiveness that the ego would have liked to satisfy upon other, extraneous individuals. The tension between the harsh super-ego and the ego that is subjected to it, is called by us the sense of guilt; it expresses itself as a need for punishment. Civilization,

therefore, obtains mastery over the individual's dangerous desire for aggression by weakening and disarming it and by setting up an agency within him to watch over it, like a garrison in a conquered city (Freud, 1930a, p. 123f.).

The transformation of destructiveness into a self-punishing conscience does not seem to be as much of an advantage as Freud implies. According to his theory conscience would have to be as cruel as the death instinct, since it is charged with its energies, and no reason is given why the death instinct should be "weakened" and "disarmed." Rather, it would seem that the following analogy expresses the real consequences of Freud's thought more logically: a city that has been ruled by a cruel enemy defeats him with the help of a dictator who then sets up a system that is just as cruel as that of the defeated enemy; and thus, what is gained?

However, this theory of the strict conscience as a manifestation of the death instinct is not the only attempt Freud makes to mitigate his concept of a tragic alternative. Another less tragic explanation is expressed in the following: "The instinct of destruction, moderated and tamed, and, as it were, inhibited in its aim, must, when it is directed towards objects, provide the ego with the satisfaction of its vital needs and with control over nature" (Freud, 1930a, p. 121). This seems to be a good example of "sublimation";* the aim of the instinct is not weakened, but it is directed toward other socially valuable aims, in this case the "control over nature."

---

*Freud did not in general use the term *sublimation* in connection with the death instinct, but it seems to me that the concept with which the following paragraph deals is the same as that which Freud calls sublimation in relation to the libido. The concept of "sublimation," however, is questionable even when Freud applied it to sexual, and especially to pregenital, instincts. In terms of the older theory, the example was popular that a surgeon uses the sublimated energy of his sadism. But is this really true? After all, the surgeon does not only cut, he also mends; and it is more likely that the best surgeons are not motivated by sublimated sadism, but by many other factors, such as having manual dexterity, the wish to heal through immediate action, the capacity for making quick decisions, et cetera.

This sounds, indeed, like a perfect solution. Man is freed from the tragic choice of destroying either others or himself, because the energy of the destructive instinct is used for the control over nature. But, we must ask, can this really be so? Can it be true that destructiveness becomes transformed into constructiveness? What can "control over nature" mean? Taming and breeding animals, gathering and cultivating plants, weaving cloth, building huts, manufacturing pottery and many more activities including the construction of machines, railroads, airplanes, skyscrapers: all these are acts of constructing, building, unifying, synthesizing, and, indeed, if one wanted to attribute them to one of the two basic instincts, they might be considered as being motivated by Eros rather than by the death instinct. With the possible exception of killing animals for their consumption and killing men in war, both of which could be considered as rooted in destructiveness, material production is not destructive but constructive.

Freud makes one other attempt to soften the harshness of his alternatives in his answer to Albert Einstein's letter on the topic "Why War?" Not even on this occasion, when confronted with the question of the psychological causes of war as posed by one of the greatest scientists and humanists of the century, did Freud try to hide or mitigate the harshness of his previous alternatives. With the fullest clarity he wrote:

> As a result of a little speculation, we have come to suppose that this instinct is at work in every living creature and is striving to bring it to ruin and to reduce life to its original condition of inanimate matter. Thus it quite seriously deserves to be called a death instinct, while the erotic instincts represent the effort to live. The death instinct turns into the destructive instinct when, with the help of special organs, it is directed outwards, on to objects. The organism preserves its own life, so to say, by destroying an extraneous one. Some portion of the death instinct, however, remains operative *within* the organism, and we have sought to trace quite a number of normal and pathological phenomena to this internalization of the destructive instinct. We have even been guilty of the heresy of attributing the origin of conscience to this

diversion inwards of aggressiveness. You will notice that it is by no means a trivial matter if this process is carried too far; it is positively unhealthy. On the other hand if these forces are turned to destruction in the external world, the organism will be relieved and the effect must be beneficial. *This would serve as a biological justification for all the ugly and dangerous impulses against which we are struggling. It must be admitted that they stand nearer to Nature than does our resistance to them for which an explanation also needs to be found* (Freud, 1933b, p. 211, italics added).

After having made this very clear and uncompromising statement summing up his previously expressed views about the death instinct, and after having stated that he could hardly believe the stories about those happy regions where there are races "who know neither coercion nor aggression," Freud tried toward the end of the letter to arrive at a less pessimistic solution than the beginning seemed to foreshadow. His hope was founded on several possibilities: "If willingness to engage in war," he wrote, "is an effect of the destructive instinct, the most obvious plan will be to bring Eros, its antagonist, into play against it. Anything that encourages the growth of emotional ties between men must operate against war" (p. 212).

It is remarkable and moving how Freud the humanist and, as he calls himself, "pacifist," tries here almost frantically to evade the logical consequences of his own premises. If the death instinct is as powerful and fundamental as Freud claims throughout, how can it be considerably reduced by bringing Eros into play, considering that they are both contained in every cell and that they constitute an irreducible quality of living matter?

Freud's second argument in favor of peace is even more fundamental. At the end of his letter to Einstein he writes:

Now war is in the crassest opposition to the psychical attitude imposed on us by the process of civilization, and for that reason we are bound to rebel against it: we simply cannot any longer put up with it. This is not merely an intellectual and emotional repudiation; we pacifists have a *constitutional* intolerance of war, an idiosyncrasy magnified, as it were, to the highest degree. It seems, indeed, as though the lowering of aesthetic standards in war plays a scarcely smaller part in our rebellion than do its cruelties. And how long shall we have to wait before the rest of mankind become pacifists too? There is no telling (p. 215).

And at the end of this letter Freud touches upon a thought found occasionally in his work, that of *the process of civilization as a factor leading to a lasting, as it were, a "constitutional," "organic" repression of instincts* (ibid.).

Freud had already expressed this view much earlier, in the *Three Essays,* when he spoke of the sharp conflict between instinct and civilization: "One gets an impression from civilized children that the construction of these dams is a product of education, and no doubt, education has much to do with it. But in reality *this development is organically determined* and fixed by heredity, and it can occasionally occur without any help at all from education" (Freud, 1905d, p. 178, italics added).

In *Civilization and Its Discontents* Freud continued this line of thinking by speaking of an "organic repression," for instance in the case of the taboo related to menstruation or anal erotism, thus paving the way to civilization. We find, even as early as 1897, Freud saying, in a letter to Fliess (November 14, 1897), that "something organic played a part in repression" (Freud, 1897, letter 75).

The various statements quoted here show that Freud's reliance on a "constitutional" intolerance to war was not only an attempt to transcend the tragic perspective of his death-instinct concept produced *ad hoc,* as it were, by his discussion with Einstein, but was in accordance with a line of thinking that, although never dominant, had been in the background of his thoughts since 1897.

If Freud's assumptions were right that civilization produces "constitutional" and hereditary repressions—that in the process of civilization certain instinctual needs are in fact weakened—then indeed he would have found a way out of the dilemma. Then civilized man would not be prompted by certain instinctual demands contrary to civilization to the same degree as primitive man. The impulse to destroy would not have the same intensity and power in civilized man as it would have in primitive man. This line of thinking would also lead to the speculation that certain inhibitions against killing might have been built up during the process of civilization and become hereditarily fixed. However, even if one could discover such hereditary factors in general, it would be exceedingly difficult to assume their existence in the case of the death instinct.

According to Freud's concept the death instinct is a tendency inherent in all living substance; it seems to be a theoretically difficult proposition to assume that this fundamental biological force could be weakened in the course of civilization. With the same logic one could assume that Eros could be constitutionally weakened, and such assumptions would lead to the more general assumption that the very nature of living substance could be altered by the process of civilization, by means of an "organic" repression.*

However this may be, today it would seem to be one of the most important subjects for research to try to establish the facts with regard to this point. Is there sufficient evidence to show that there has been a constitutional, organic repression of certain instinctual demands in the course of civilization? Is this repression one that is different from repression in Freud's usual sense, inasmuch as it weakens the instinctual demand, rather than removing it from consciousness or diverting it to other aims? And more specifically, in the course of history have man's destructive impulses become weaker, or have inhibitory impulses developed that are now hereditarily fixed? To answer this question would require extended studies, especially in anthropology, sociopsychology and genetics.

Perhaps the puzzle of Freud's self-deception about the validity

---

*What speaks most against Freud's assumption is that prehistoric man was not more but less aggressive than civilized man.

of the concept of the death instinct requires still another element for its solution. Every careful reader of Freud's work must also be aware of how tentatively and cautiously he treated his new theoretical constructions when presenting them for the first time. He made no claim for their validity and sometimes even spoke deprecatingly of their value. But the more time passed, the more hypothetical constructs turned into theories upon which new constructions and theories were built. Freud the theorist was very well aware of the doubtful validity of many of his constructs. Why did he forget these original doubts? It is hard to answer this question; one possible answer may be found in his role as the leader of the psychoanalytic movement (see Fromm, 1959a). Those of his students who dared to criticize fundamental aspects of his theories left him or were squeezed out in one way or another. Those who built the movement were mostly pedestrian men, from the standpoint of their theoretical capacity, and it would have been difficult for them to follow Freud through basic theoretical changes. They needed a dogma in which they believed and around which they could organize the movement.* Thus Freud the scientist became to some extent the prisoner of Freud the leader of the movement; or to put it differently, Freud the teacher became the prisoner of his faithful, but uncreative disciples.

*This is borne out by the reaction of the majority of Freudians to the death instinct. They could not follow this new and profound speculation and found a way out by formulating Freud's ideas about aggression in terms of the old instinct theory.

5. Why Was Psychoanalysis Transformed from a Radical Theory to One of Adaptation?

While Freud cannot be considered a "radical" even in the widest political meaning of the word—in fact he was a typical liberal with strong conservative features—his *theory* was undeniably radical. His theory of sex was not radical, nor were his metapsychological speculations, but his insistence on the central role of repression and the fundamental significance of the unconscious sector of our mental life can be called radical. This theory was radical because it attacked the last fortress of man's belief in his omnipotence and omniscience, the belief in his conscious thought as an ultimate datum of human experience. Galileo had deprived man of the illusion that the earth was the center of the world, Darwin of the illusion that he was created by God, but nobody had questioned that his conscious thinking was the last datum on which he could rely. Freud deprived man of his pride in his rationality. He went to the roots—that is what "radical" literally means—and discovered that a great deal of our conscious thinking only veils our real thoughts and feelings and hides the truth; most of our conscious thought is a sham, a mere rationalization of thoughts and desires which we prefer not to be aware of.

Freud's discovery was potentially revolutionary because it could have led people to open their eyes to the reality of the structure of the society they live in and hence to the wish to change it in accordance with the interests and desires of the vast majority. But while Freud's thought had such revolutionary potential, its wide acceptance did not lead to manifestations of this potential. While the main attack of his colleagues and the public was a thrust against the views on sex, which violated certain taboos of the nineteenth-century European middle class, his discovery of the unconscious had no revolutionary consequences. This is actually not surprising. To demand directly or indirectly greater tolerance toward sex was essentially in the line of other liberal causes, such as greater tolerance for criminals and a more liberal attitude toward children, and so forth. The concentration on sex actually deflected from the criticism of society and hence had in fact partly a politically reactionary function. If the incapacity to solve one's sexual problems was at the bottom of the general malaise, there was no need for a critical examination of the economic, social and political factors that stood in the way of the full growth of the individual. On the contrary, political radicalism could be understood as a sign of neurosis because, for Freud and most of his students, the liberal bourgeois was the paradigm of the healthy man. One tried to explain radicalism of the left or of the right as outcomes of neurotic processes, as for instance the Oedipus complex, and *prima facie* a political belief which was not that of the liberal middle class was suspected of being "neurotic."

The vast majority of psychoanalysts were of the same urban intellectual middle class from which the bulk of their patients came. Hardly more than a handful of psychoanalysts had radical beliefs. The best known among them was Wilhelm Reich, who thought that inhibition of sex creates antirevolutionary characters and that sexual freedom would create revolutionary characters. Hence he formulated a theory that sexual liberation leads to revolutionary orientation. Of course Reich was quite wrong, as later developments showed. This sexual liberation was largely part of the ever-increasing consumerism. If people were taught to spend and spend, rather than, as in the nineteenth century, to save and save, if they were transformed into "consumers," one had not only to permit but encourage sexual consumption. It is after all the most simple and the cheapest of all consumption. Reich was misled because at his time the conservatives had a strict sexual morality and he concluded from this that sexual liberty would lead to an anticonservative, revolutionary attitude. Historical development has shown that sexual liberation served the development of consumerism and if anything weakened political radicalism. Unfortunately Reich knew and understood little of Marx and could be called a "sexual anarchist."

In still another aspect Freud thought as a child of his time. He was a member of a class society in which a small minority monopolized most of the riches and defended its supremacy by the use of power and thought control over those it ruled. Freud, taking this type of society for granted, constructed a model of man's mind along the same lines. The "id," symbolizing the uneducated masses, had to be controlled by the ego, the rational elite. If Freud could have imagined a classless and free society he would have dispensed with the ego and id as universal categories of the human mind.

In my opinion the danger of a reactionary function of psychoanalysis can only be overcome by uncovering the unconscious factors in political and religious ideologies.* Marx in his interpretation of bourgeois ideology did essentially for society what

---

*The Soviet Communists have criticized Freud for his lack of attention to pathogenic social factors. In my opinion this is a convenient rationalization. In a system which is centered on preventing the citizen from being aware of what the reality of the system is, and that relies entirely on the brainwashing of its citizens with illusions, the criticism of psychoanalysis is in reality not directed against its lack of giving proper significance to social factors, but against its radical attempt to help men to see the reality behind the illusions.

Freud did for the individual. But it has been widely neglected that Marx outlined a psychology of his own that avoided Freud's errors and is the basis of a socially oriented psychoanalysis. He distinguished between instincts which are innate, such as sex and hunger, and those passions like ambition, hate, hoarding, exploitativeness, et cetera, which are produced by the practice of life and in the last analysis by the productive forces existing in a certain society, and hence can be subject to change in the historical process.*

The taming of psychoanalysis and its transformation from a radical into a liberal theory of adjustment could hardly have been avoided, not only because the practitioners came from the bourgeois middle classes, but also the patients. What most of the patients wanted was not to become more human, more free, more independent—and that would have meant more critical and revolutionary-minded—but to suffer no more than the average member of their class. They did not want to be free men but successful bourgeois and did not want to pay the radical price that the change from the predominance of having over that of being would have required. Why should they? They hardly saw a really happy person, only a few people who had succeeded in being relatively satisfied with their lot, especially if they were successful and admired by others. This was the model they were striving to achieve and the psychoanalyst, in playing the role of the model, assumed that the patient would become like him if he only talked for a long enough time. Naturally, quite a few people, having a sympathetic listener to talk to, felt better, aside from the fact that as years go by experience in living makes the average person improve his lot, except those who are too sick to learn from experience.

Some politically naïve people may think that if analysis is a radical theory it must be popular with the Communists and especially in the so-called "Socialist countries." Indeed it had a cer-

*See Marx, *Economic and Philosophical Manuscripts of 1844.*

tain popularity at the beginning of the revolution (for instance, Trotsky himself was interested in psychoanalysis and particularly in Adler's theory), but that was true only as long as the Soviet Union still had elements of a revolutionary system. With the ascendancy of Stalinism and the change from a revolutionary to a thoroughly conservative and reactionary society which the Soviet Union still is today, the popularity of psychoanalysis diminished to the point of disappearance. The Soviet critique is that it is idealistic, ignores economic and social factors, is bourgeois; and many more critical points are made, some of which are not without merit. But to hold them against psychoanalysis is mere sham if they are made by the Soviet ideologists. What they cannot stand in psychoanalysis is not any of these defects but its one great achievement—namely, critical thinking and the distrust of ideologies.

Unfortunately, psychoanalysis has lost much of its critical sting. By concentrating mainly on the individual, and especially on the events of early childhood, it has deflected attention from socioeconomic factors.

Psychoanalysts generally have followed the trends of bourgeois thinking. They adopted the philosophy of their class and for all practical purposes became supporters of consumerism. While Freud did not say so, his teaching was distorted into meaning that neurosis was the result of lack of sexual satisfaction (caused by repression)—hence that full sexual satisfaction was a condition of mental health. Victory of consumerism on all fronts!

Freud's formulations had another and very severe flaw: the ambiguity of the term *reality*. Freud, like most members of his class, considered contemporary capitalist society to be the highest, most developed form of social structure. It was "reality," while all other social structures were either more primitive or utopian. Today only opinion-producers and politicians subject to their suggestions believe this or pretend to believe it. An ever-growing number of people has become aware that capitalist society is just one of innumerable social structures and is neither more nor less "real" than the societies of Central African tribes.

Freud believed that the practice of what he called "perversions"—all not-strictly-genital sexual activities—was incompatible with highly civilized life. Since the sexual practices of bourgeois marriage excluded all "perversion" as violation of the "dignity" of the bourgeois wife, he had to arrive at the tragic conclusion that full happiness and full civilization excluded each other.

Freud was a genius at making constructions and it may not be too farfetched to attribute to him the motto "Constructions Make Reality." In this respect he shows an affinity with two sources with which he was not actually familiar: the Talmud and Hegel's philosophy.

Bibliography

Ammacher, P. 1962. "On the Significance of Freud's Neurological Background." In *Psychological Issues.* Seattle: University of Washington Press.

Benveniste, E. 1966. *Problèmes de Linguistique Général,* Paris: Gallimard.

Fenichel, O. 1945. "Criticism of the Concept of a Death Instinct." In *The Collected Papers of Otto Fenichel,* 2 Vols. Vol. 1, pp. 59–61. New York: W. W. Norton.

Freud, S. 1950. *Aus den Anfaengen der Psychoanalyse.* London: Imago.

——1897. *"Letter to Fliess"(14 November, 1897).* In *Aus den Anfaengen der Psychoanalyse,* pp. 244–49 (trans. *Origins of Psychoanalysis: Letters to Wilhelm Fliess, Draft S and Note S, 1887–1902.* Pp. 244–49. Edited by Marie Bonaparte et al. 1954. Basic Books.)

——1953–74. *The Standard Edition of the Complete Psychological Works of Sigmund Freud.* Vols. 1–24, London: The Hogarth Press. *Complete Psychological Works,* 24 Volumes. New York: 1964. Macmillan.

——1898b. *The Psychical Mechanism of Forgetfulness.* S.E. Vol. 3, pp. 287–97.

——1899a. *Screen Memories.* S.E. Vol. 3, pp. 301–22.

——1900a. *The Interpretation of Dreams.* S.E. Vols. 4 and 5.

——1905d. *Three Essays on the Theory of Sexuality.* S.E. Vol. 7, pp. 123–243.

————1905e. *Fragment of an Analysis of a Case of Hysteria.* S.E. Vol. 7, pp. 1–122.

————1907b. *The Psychopathology of Everyday Life.* S.E. Vol. 6.

————1908b. *Character and Anal Eroticism.* S.E. Vol. 9, pp. 167–75.

————1908d. *"Civilized" Sexual Morality and Modern Nervous Illness.* S.E. Vol. 9, pp. 179–204.

————1914c. *On Narcissism: An Introduction.* S.E. Vol. 14. pp. 67–102.

————1916–17. *Introductory Lectures on Psychoanalysis.* S.E. Vols. 15 and 16.

————1918b. *From the History of an Infantile Neurosis.* S.E. Vol. 17, pp. 1–122.

————1920g. *Beyond the Pleasure Principle.* S.E. Vol. 18, pp. 1–64.

————1921c. *Group Psychology and the Analysis of the Ego.* S.E. Vol. 18, pp. 65–143.

————1923b. *The Ego and the Id.* S.E. Vol. 19, pp. 1–66.

————1924c. *The Economic Problem of Masochism.* S.E. Vol. 19, pp. 155–70.

————1925e. *The Resistance to Psycho-Analysis.* S.E. Vol. 19, pp. 213–22.

————1926d. *Inhibitions, Symptoms and Anxiety.* S.E. Vol. 20, pp. 75–172.

————1926e. *The Question of Lay Analysis.* S.E. Vol. 20, p. 177–250.

————1930a. *Civilization and Its Discontents.* S.E. Vol. 21, pp. 57–145.

————1933a. *New Introductory Lectures on Psycho-Analysis.* S.E. Vol. 22, pp. 1–182.

————1933b. *Why War?* S.E. Vol. 22, pp. 195–215.

————1937c. *Analysis Terminable and Interminable.* S.E. Vol. 23, pp. 209–53.

————1940a. *An Outline of Psycho-Analysis.* S.E. Vol. 23, pp. 139–207.

Fromm, E. 1932a. "The Method and Function of an Analytic Psychoanalysis." In *The Crisis of Psychoanalysis.* New York: Holt, Rinehart and Winston, 1970.

————1941a. *Escape from Freedom,* New York: Farrar and Rinehart.

————1951a. *The Forgotten Language: An Introduction to the Understanding of Dreams, Fairy Tales and Myths.* New York: Rinehart.

————1955a. *The Sane Society.* New York: Rinehart.

————1959a. *Sigmund Freud's Mission: An Analysis of His Personality and Influence.* New York: Harper.

————1963e. "C. G. Jung: Prophet of the Unconscious. A Discussion of 'Memories, Dreams, Reflexions' by C. G. Jung." Recorded and edited by Aniella Jaffé, *Scientific American* 209:283–90.

————1968h. "Marx's Contribution to the Knowledge of Man." *Social Science Information* 7, no. 3, pp. 7–17.

————1973a. *The Anatomy of Human Destructiveness.* New York: Holt, Rinehart and Winston.

————1976a. *To Have or to Be?* New York and London: Harper and Row.

Gardiner, M. (ed.). 1971. *The Wolf-Man by the Wolf-Man,* Supplement by Ruth Mack Brunswick. New York: Basic Books.

Holt, R. R. 1965. "A Review of Some of Freud's Biological Assumptions and Their Influence on His Theories." In N. S. Greenfield and W. C. Lewis (eds.), *Psychoanalysis and Current Biological Thought,* pp. 93–124. Madison: University of Wisconsin Press.

Jones, E. 1957. *The Life and Work of Sigmund Freud,* 3 Vols., New York: Basic Books.

Pratt, J. 1958. "Epilegomena to the Study of Freudian Instinct Theory." *International Journal of Psychoanalysis* 39:17 ff.

Robert, C. 1915: *Ödipus.* Berlin: Weidmannsche Buchhandlung.

Schachtel, E. 1947. "Memory and Childhood Amnesia." *Psychiatry* 10, no. 1.

Schneidewin, F. W. 1852. "Die Sage vom Ödipus." In *Abhandlungen der Koeniglichen Gesellschaft der Wissenschaften zu Goettingen.* Vol. 5. Göettingen: Dieterich.

Sophocles. 1955. *Oedipus Rex.* In *Seven Famous Greek Plays.* Edited by Whitney J. Oates and Eugene O'Neill. Translated by R. C. Webb. New York: Random House.

Index

About the Author

Psychoanalyst, social critic, moral philosopher, ERICH FROMM was born in Frankfurt, Germany, in 1900. He sought American citizenship after visiting the United States in 1933 and emigrated from Germany, then dominated by the Nazis, in 1934. He trained in philosophy, sociology and psychology at the University of Heidelberg, receiving a doctorate in philosophy at the age of 22, and thus bringing a nonmedical background to his subsequent studies at the Berlin Psychoanalytic Institute. After emigrating to America, he helped found the William Alanson White Institute for Psychiatry, Psychoanalysis and Psychology in New York City, and was a trustee and teacher there for many years, while maintaining an active practice. He lectured all over the world and held formal faculty appointments at Columbia University, Bennington College, Yale University, Michigan State University, New York University and the National University of Mexico. The author of some twenty books, including *Escape from Freedom, The Art of Loving* and *The Sane Society,* he described the dehumanizing effects of contemporary society, and developed the concepts of alienation and self-awareness that have become part of the consciousness of our times. As a psychoananyst, Dr. Fromm is generally considered a "neo-Freudian," one who, in contrast to the biological pessimism of Freud, believes in the potential of man's unique faculties—imagination, reason, will—to overcome unconscious forces. His last book, *Greatness and Limitations of Freud's Thought,* is a loving critique of Freud's theories. Dr. Fromm died at his home in Muralto, Switzerland, in March 1980.